Harold W. Dickhut is president of Management Counselors, Inc., of Chicago. He served as general manager of Stivers Lifesavers, Inc., a national temporary-help service, and has been executive vice president of Automation Institute, a Chicago business school. His professional teaching experience includes teaching posts at North Park College and the Metropolitan School of Business of Chicago, Roosevelt University, and Northwestern University.

HAROLD W. DICKHUT

THE PROFESSIONAL RESUME & JOB SEARCH GUIDE

PRENTICE HALL PRESS · NEW YORK

To William C. Jakes

Published by Prentice Hall Press
A Division of Simon & Schuster, Inc.
Gulf + Western Building
One Gulf + Western Plaza
New York, NY 10023

Originally published by Prentice-Hall, Inc.

PRENTICE HALL PRESS is a trademark of Simon & Schuster, Inc.

Library of Congress Cataloging-in-Publication Data

Dickhut, Harold W
  The professional resume and job search guide.

  First-4th ed. published under title: Professional
resume/job search guide.
  Bibliography: p.
  Includes index.
  1. Résumés (Employment) 2. Applications for
positions. 3. Employment interviewing. I. Title.
HF5383.D47 1981   650.1′4   80-15824
ISBN 0-13-725705-8 (pbk.)
ISBN 0-13-725713-9

Manufactured in the United States of America

20 19 18 17 16 15 14 13 12

First Prentice Hall Press Edition

contents

section 1

how to use the resume & job search guide

Introduction

Today, a good resume is a requirement for any individual seeking a position. It is step number one in any job search. The time and money you spend to prepare one is a worthwhile investment for you and could prove to be of tremendous value.

If you are changing jobs out of necessity . . . just looking to improve your position . . . a business or a vocational school student . . . just graduating from college . . . returning from military service . . . THEN, this Resume/Job Search Guide is for you.

Prepared by Management Counselors, Inc., Chicago, this Guide is based on the solid experience of working with many hundreds of men and women in professional resume preparation, position search activities, job counsel and placement. Years of successful experience in job guidance are brought together in this Guide, so that you can have the advantages of this extended knowledge in the preparation of your own individual resume.

Another big personal advantage to working diligently on your resume, over and above the obvious usefulness it has in your job search, is this. By the very discipline required to prepare your data prior to writing, you have the opportunity for some personal evaluation of yourself. Further, with all your past employment and/or educational history at your fingertips, you are now better prepared to handle yourself during employment interviews.

Two words of encouragement—and caution. First, your resume will be only as good as you can make it. Read this Guide carefully—all the essentials are here. Second, remember that a resume by itself, no matter how well prepared, will not get you a new job. It is a key sales tool for you and will open some doors. And that is exactly what it is intended to do.

What Your Resume Is and What It Does

Consider for a moment what a resume is and what it is intended to do. Simply stated, a resume is your representative, your image; it is YOU when you aren't there. It's a summary of your personal data, your educational background and training, your business or professional experience and qualifications, your achievement highlights and very important, your *objective*.

Your resume is intended to be a word picture of you . . . designed not only to give a potential employer your factual data, but to create an impression with him.

An impression of your desirability for him, and to stimulate action on his part toward setting up an interview. Or, perhaps, to talk to you on the phone.

Your resume, by itself, will *not* get you a job. You have to do that yourself. It will usually open the door and favorably pave the way. However, remember that your resume must reflect *you*, and it cannot effectively portray what you are *not*. But, it surely can show what you want to do, how your past experience is applicable to that goal, and all the other pertinent things about you.

Your resume is a SALES TOOL for you to use in marketing yourself. It is not your whole life history, not even necessarily your entire employment history. It is not an application blank.

Keep in mind that a resume should be 100% honest, conservative and all statements should be positive. Avoid the negative approach in all your phraseology.

Be concise. The employer who reads your resume does not want to study long resumes—or long paragraphs in short resumes. Keep your statements to one or two lines whenever possible.

Remember the value of "white space" so that your resume is easy to read. At all times, think and write through the eyes of the employer. He or she is the person you want to influence—to interest enough so that you will be called in for an interview.

Preparing Your Resume

Are you ready to begin? Then start. Prepare your resume by following this Guide step by step as outlined in Sections II thru VIII.

Step 1. Collect and organize your data, similar to the completed Data Sheets example in Section II.

Step 2. Use the check lists in Sections IV and V.

Step 3. Study the sample resumes.

Step 4. Prepare the first draft, then the final draft.

Step 5. Type your resume for printing.

Step 6. Get quality printing.

You now have your SALES TOOL. Begin your Search!

section 2

organizing your resume material

Instructions for Listing Your Material in the Data Sheet Format

NAME AND ADDRESS: Present yourself by the name you ordinarily use in your business and personal life. If you usually use your first name and a middle initial, do so in your resume. First names spelled out are better than initials. If your name is George William Cook, III but you are known as George W. Cook, use the latter. Nicknames are best avoided except in unusual cases.

Your address should be shown in full: street number and name, with Street, Road, Drive, Avenue or Lane included. Spell out both city and state. Include the zip code.

Normally, use just your home phone. If you feel safe in doing so, include your current work phone, but this makes your resume out of date as soon as you leave your present job. In any case, be sure to include the area code.

If you have a temporary address and/or phone number, you can include this at the top of your resume, in addition to or in place of your regular or permanent address, depending on circumstances.

1. OBJECTIVE: State the position you seek in very concise terms in as few words as possible. Try to make it comprehensive, though, so that it can cover several related areas if you have such an objective. It is best not to include too many objectives, or widely diversified objectives, in the same resume.

   In some cases, it may be best to eliminate the objective entirely. For example, you may want to search in two or three widely separated fields. You have a choice of omitting the objective, or of creating several resumes, each one geared to fit one area or specific goal.

2. AREAS OF KNOWLEDGE/EXPERIENCE: Refer to separate Section IV for instructions in preparing this portion.

3. PERSONAL: This is largely self explanatory. Generally, it is adequate simply to show Health as "Good" or "Excellent." If you need to use crutches, just say so. Give the number of children, but their ages are not necessary. If your children are grown, or your family exceptionally large, say "Family."

   Use your actual birthdate, rather than age, to avoid making your resume obsolete after your next birthday.

   If you are over 55, consider just omitting any reference at all to age or birthdate.

   If you are over 50, the "Personal" items can be shown on the last page of your resume rather than on the first.

4. EDUCATION: If you have attended college, it is not necessary to show the name of your High School. A young person just out of High School will want to list his

school. If you did not attend any college or business school, then it may be best to eliminate the "Education" area entirely, unless your Special Training Courses are quite heavy. If they are, and are pertinent to the work you do or seek, list them under a SPECIAL TRAINING heading.

Degrees can be shown in reverse chronological order with the highest degree listed first. With one degree acquired by attending several schools, show first the school granting the degree, followed by the other schools and then list the degree itself. With attendance at several schools but no degree, list first the school with the highest reputation.

If you are a student, graduate student or a recent college graduate (last 2-3 years), you may want to add additional sections to your resume just below Education. The first you can title *Educational Highlights* or *College Training.* The second may be headed *Student Activities.* Refer to Section III of this Guide, and to the appropriate sample resumes in Section VI.

5. PROFESSIONAL STATUS AND MEMBERSHIPS: Certification refers to "CPA" in Accounting, "CLU" in Insurance, "CPS" for Certified Professional Secretary, "Registered Engineer, State of _____" in Engineering. Other examples are AIA, CPM, CSM. Also, "Licensed to practice Law: State of _____."

List the names of key professional or trade associations in which you hold, or recently held, memberships. Include any officerships held, or important committee chairmanships.

6. SALARY: You have a choice. Show a range such as $9,000-$10,000 or $18,000-$20,000 or any range that will be reasonable in the eyes of the employer. If your salary requirements are truly negotiable, say "Open to discussion, depending on position and potential."

If your salary needs are in the higher brackets, at $20,000 or more, it is often best *not* to show any specific amounts. If necessary, handle a direct request for the information in your cover letter.

7. TRAVEL: State your willingness to travel on the job. It's best to be willing to travel any amount required by the position.

8. LOCATE: Say whether you are readily willing to relocate, willing for the right potential, or prefer to remain in your present area.

9. MILITARY: This item is normally included to show status, reserve status or service completed. If you have completed military service, or are in an Active Reserve, say so. Omit the item completely if you have not been in service.

10. AVAILABILITY: If unemployed, or you can report in 10 days, say "Immediate." Usually, it's best to show "2 weeks' notice required" or "30 days' notice required" or whatever the case may be. In any event, you must indicate your willingness to give your present employer adequate notice.

11. PRESENT EMPLOYER CONTACT: Indicate whether or not your current employer is aware of your decision to change, or consider a change, and may or may not be contacted at this time.

12. BUSINESS REFERENCES: Simply state that they are available upon request. It is normally better not to list them in your resume, because addresses, titles, phone numbers and company affiliations are subject to change.

13. INTERESTS and ACTIVITIES: A limited number of hobbies, interests, avocations may be shown, especially if relevant to your Objective. If space is a problem, omit this item.

14. COMMUNITY SERVICES: Not vital, but may be included. Omit references to religious denomination.

15. FOREIGN LANGUAGES: Include only if pertinent to past work or present objective.

16. FOREIGN TRAVEL: Include only if pertinent to past work or present objective.

17. WORK EXPERIENCE: Your work experience is best shown in reverse chronological order, that is, with your current position (or latest position, if unemployed) shown first. Follow that with the second latest position and so on back to your initial position.

    Make out a sheet for each *company, organization, firm* or *agency* (if only one position held) or for each *position* held within each employer organization.

    Technically, you should include *all* employers and account for your time completely since leaving school or completing military service. However, short term jobs or brief periods of unemployment may be excluded. Also, early work experiences not relevant to your present position or field, can be lumped by either showing just the positions held, or the employer organization names.

    (a) **Employer and Size:** List the name of the organization, size and a one-sentence description of its activities.

    (b) **Position Held:** Show your position by title.

    (c) **Earnings:** Salary or earnings deserves your special attention. Expert opinion on the subject seems to be divided. If your earnings over the years have increased in a regular progression, it may be advisable to show this, especially if current earnings are below $15,000.

    If your earnings are more substantial, or you desire to negotiate up or down, you may want to omit all reference to the subject in your resume. Should you be answering an ad requesting salary history, you can always handle this in your cover letter.

    (d) **Responsibilities:** Be brief in stating your job responsibilities. Eliminate all minor details. List 3 or 4 major responsibilities.

    (e) **Achievements:** List in concise fashion your outstanding or principal accomplishments while in that position. Be concise, using one or two lines or senences to state the facts or the results.

    Often, the "Achievements" sections under each employer listing become the real heart of the resume. Your achievements are what you actually *did* for a past employer which built his sales, increased his profit, reduced his costs or effectively did his research or administered his departments.

An employer is thinking as he reads your resume: "What did this individual do that made or saved a dollar, which perhaps he can do for me." Put another way, the business employer is usually looking for a results-oriented employee who has one eye on profit potential for the company.

Responsibilities of a Sales Manager can easily be quite similar in countless companies. What separates top performers from other managers is the *profitable* sales results they achieve.

Make full use of the "thought starter" check lists provided as guides in Section V, in writing up your achievements.

(f) **Reason for Change:** Your statement under Reason for Change should be a reasonable presentation, very briefly stated, of why you are considering leaving, or why you resigned or were terminated. Do not make statements which put past employers in a bad light. Dishonesty has no place in your resume, and your reasons for leaving are no exception. If there is simply no way to explain an adverse reason in print, or briefly, it's best to just omit the item entirely.

RESUME DATA SHEET

Name: *HAROLD M. SANDS*
Street Address: *313 Wooddale Drive*
City and State: *Norman, Oklahoma*
Telephone No.: *236-0056*

Zip Code: *73069*
Area Code: *405*

1. <u>Objective</u> (Position Desired): *Sales (eventually management) industrial products*

2. <u>Areas of Knowledge and Experience:</u>
   (List 12 to 20 one or two word phrases which concisely describe your experience areas)

   Sales
   Selling Key Accounts
   New Product Exposure
   Distributor Set-up,
   Control, Training
   National Account Sales
   Territory Layout

   Pricing
   Customer Service
   Complaint Handling
   Plant Surveys
   Sales Personnel-
   Hire, Train
   Sales Supervision

   Forecasts
   Budgets
   Promotions
   Trade Shows
   Marketing
   Distribution

3. <u>Personal:</u> Birthdate: *March 15, 1940*   Health: *Excellent*
   Height: *5'11"*   Marital Status: *Married*
   Weight: *185 lbs.*   Children (number): *2*

4. <u>Education:</u> College (name, city and state, years completed):
   University of Denver, Denver, Colo.

   Degree: *B.A. — 1963*

   Major: *Business Adm.* Minor: *Marketing*

   Graduate School (name, city and state, years, degree):
   U. of Denver
   Sales Analysis — Principles of Marketing
   Special Training Courses (apart from above):

5. <u>Professional Status and Memberships:</u>
   Professional and Trade Association Memberships:
   American Industrial Hygiene Assn.
   Sales Executives
   Certification:

6. <u>Salary:</u>   Acceptable salary range in new position;
                    or, your decision to omit this item entirely.
                    Open - in present range - potential important

7. <u>Travel:</u>   Extent of on-the-job travelling acceptable in new
                    position: *Whatever necessary*

8. <u>Locate:</u>   Agreeable to relocating? *Yes*

9. <u>Military:</u>   Service, Rank, Dates: ___

                    Reserve Status: ___

10. <u>Availability:</u>   Immediate or Extent of "Notice" Required:
                    3 weeks required

11. <u>Present Employer Contact:</u>
                    Is he aware of this prospective job change? *No*

                    May he be contacted at this time? *No*

12. <u>Business References:</u>
                    Generally, references are not listed in the resume
                    itself. A statement is made that references are
                    available upon request.

13. <u>Interests and Activities:</u>
                    Hobbies, avocations, non-business pursuits:

                    Golf   *Swimming*
                    Bowling   *Gardening*
                    Photography   *Travel*

14. <u>Community Services:</u>
                    Offices - Organizations
                    Boy Scouts of America: Scoutmaster
                    Parent Teachers Assn: President

15. <u>Foreign Languages:</u> (read, write, speak, fluency)
                    German - read & write
                    speak moderate

16. <u>Foreign Travel:</u>
                    List countries visited on business trips, or in
                    extensive personal travel.
                    Europe - Middle East - Orient

17. **Experience:**   EMPLOYER NAME _Household Products, Inc._
                      ADDRESS _Norman, Oklahoma_

(a)   From _1973_   Type of Organization: _Mfg. industrial soaps,_
      To _Present_   _hand cleaners, lotions, industrial_
                           Size of Organization: _cleaners._
                           Approx. Annual Sales Volume $ _2 million_
                                          or Budget $
                           Approx. Number of Employees:

(b)   <u>Position Held:</u>   _District Manager_

(c)   <u>Earnings:</u>   Top Base Salary: _$19,000_
                         Supplementary (Bonus, Profit Sharing)
                         bonus, car, expenses

(d)   <u>Responsibilities:</u>

Sell Fortune "500" Accounts.
Promote new products. Service national
accounts. Set up distributors, select, train
— hold meetings. Follow up.
Supervise 10 sales representatives in
6-state area. Hire, train.

(e)   <u>Achievements:</u>

Set up major distributor. First year's
business $60,000. First 3 month's sales
1975 25% over first 3 months last year.
Good liaison — retained almost 100% of
business already established in area.
Total area sales first 3 months this
year increased 10% over last year.
Only area to go over quota last year.
(nationwide)

(f)   <u>Reason for Change:</u>
More opportunity to progress in
management.

17. **Experience:**   EMPLOYER NAME   *Household Products, Inc.*
                                  ADDRESS   *Norman, Oklahoma*

(a)   From *1970*   Type of Organization:

            To *1972*   Size of Organization:

                                 Approx. Annual Sales Volume $
                                              or Budget $
                                 Approx. Number of Employees:

(b)   Position Held: *Sales Representative*

(c)   Earnings: Top Base Salary: *$12,500*

                        Supplementary (Bonus, Profit Sharing) *Bonus and expenses*

(d)   Responsibilities:

Sell all products to industrial companies, hospitals, schools and other institutions. Customer contact — orders, pricing, delivery. Keep customers informed of new products.

(e)   Achievements:

No. 1 salesman in Area (10 salesmen) in 1972.

Added 22 new accounts.

1970 — received "Highest Performance" rating in Company's New Representative category.

(f)   Reason for Change: *Promotion.*

17. Experience: EMPLOYER NAME *Western Paper Products Co.*
ADDRESS *Denver, Colorado*

(a) From *1965*   Type of Organization: *Paper cups and containers*

To *1969*   Size of Organization:

Approx. Annual Sales Volume $
or Budget $
Approx. Number of Employees:

(b) Position Held: *Sales Representative*

(c) Earnings: Top Base Salary: *$12,000*
Supplementary (Bonus, Profit Sharing)

(d) Responsibilities:

Cold canvass calls
Maintain present accounts.
Sell to distributors, food processors,
restaurants, schools, hospitals,
service food caterers.

(e) Achievements:

Promoted new line to unrelated industries
— resulted in expansion of sales:
Introduced coffee service cup with
plastic holder — now being used
extensively.
Added 14 new accounts in one year.

(f) Reason for Change: *More opportunity.*

17. Experience: EMPLOYER NAME *Western Paper Products Co.*

ADDRESS *Denver, Colo.*

(a)   From *1963*   Type of Organization:

To *1965*   Size of Organization:

Approx. Annual Sales Volume $
or Budget $

Approx. Number of Employees:

(b)   Position Held: *Sales Trainee*

(c)   Earnings: Top Base Salary: *$9,000*

Supplementary (Bonus, Profit Sharing)

(d)   Responsibilities:

Sell new customers.
Service and sell present accounts.
Get to know complete Company
line of products.

(e)   Achievements:

(f)   Reason for Change: *Promotion.*

section 3

special guidelines for student resumes

If you are now or have recently been a college, business college or business school graduate or a student without a Bachelor's or Associate Degree, and your actual work experience ranges from none to a year or two, the material in this Section will help *you* to prepare a better resume. Similarly, if you just finished military service, the major points apply.

The importance of preparing a good resume can't be stressed too much. Most of the time, the resume *is* you, and represents you in your absence. A good resume that is accurate, complete and neat can do a lot in creating the best impression on a prospective employer. Your resume must be designed to *sell* you to an employer. It should appeal to him, and to his interests, rather than to emphasize your desires.

Every individual has some strong points and some weak ones. Your work experience will be limited, usually, so you will want to make the most of your educational background. However, if you have good summer work experience, it's a plus if it is at all oriented toward your objective. Another plus is to have returned to the same company for several summers. And, show promotions if possible, either in the same company or in higher levels of work with different companies.

What's needed is really some careful, objective soul searching to determine your abilities and interests, and then stress them as they relate to educational success, work experience and job objective.

Prepare a special section for your data sheet called EDUCATIONAL HIGH-LIGHTS, and include the material under this heading right below the EDUCATION section of your final product. Consider the following example from the resume of a recent college graduate seeking an entry position in business or government.

EDUCATIONAL HIGHLIGHTS   UNDERGRADUATE TRAINING

Political Science
American Government
Political Theory
Public Administration
Political Parties and
   Pressure Groups
Methods of Political Science

International Relations
International Relations
American Foreign Policy
European Governments

Speech
Public Speaking
Discussion
Acting
Stagecraft

English
English I
Types of Fiction
Expository Writing

Economics
Principles of Economics

Notice how only certain selected subjects are included. These are *highlights*. Full course names or numbers are not necessary.

Here is how a current MBA presented his educational credentials, both at the graduate and undergraduate levels.

EDUCATIONAL HIGHLIGHTS
NORTHWESTERN UNIVERSITY, EVANSTON, ILLINOIS
GRADUATE SCHOOL OF MANAGEMENT
Areas of concentration: Finance, Accounting

Finance
Investments
Money Markets
Financial Management
Investment Portfolio
  Management
Security Analysis

Related Courses:
Economics (Micro and Macro)
Management and the Computer
Business Policy
Business Forecasting

Accounting
Cost Accounting
Contemporary Issues in
  Accounting
Mergers and Acquisitions
Information Systems for
  Management Control
Information Planning Criteria

UNDERGRADUATE TRAINING

Finance
Business Law
Insurance
Corporation Finance

Accounting
Principles of Accounting
Managerial Accounting
Data Processing

Management
Principles of Management
Production
Personnel

Marketing
Marketing and the Economy
Marketing and the Firm
Salesmanship

A Law student, preparing his resume well in advance of receiving his Juris Doctor degree, presented his law school and undergraduate highlights this way:

**EDUCATIONAL
HIGHLIGHTS**

JOHN MARSHALL LAW SCHOOL

Practice Court
Actual preparation and trial of a case, including drafting and serving process and pleadings and pre-trial and post-trial motions.

Property Settlements
Study of nature of estates in real and personal property and the impact of Federal and State taxes on the estates. Preparation of an estate plan.

Workmen's Compensation
Lawyers Institute course examining the Illinois Workmen's Compensation practice and procedure.

UNDERGRADUATE STUDIES

Management
Fundamentals of Professional
  Management
Business Correspondence
Business Statistics
Production Management
Personnel Administration
Business Organizations
Policy Formulation and
  Administration

Accounting
Principles of Accounting
Administrative Accounting
Cost Accounting

Economics
Macro, Micro
Social Control of Business
Labor Economics and
  Organization

Finance
Financial Structures
Money and Banking
Business Finance
Investments

Marketing
Principles of Marketing
Advertising

For business college, community college, business school and correspondence school graduates and students, exactly the same principles apply. For example, a business school graduate handled his educational training this way.

EDUCATIONAL TRAINING   METROPOLITAN SCHOOL OF BUSINESS, Chicago, Ill.
AA Degree. 42 hours of Accounting.

Accounting
Introductory Accounting
Intermediate Accounting
Advanced Accounting
Cost Accounting

Government Accounting
Auditing
Federal, State Taxes
Automation Accounting

Data Processing

Business Administration
Business Management
Business Law
Personnel Management

Economics
Money and Banking
Finance

Mathematics, Statistics
Business Writing
Business Machines
   10 Key Calculators
   Typewriting

If your educational training has been vocational oriented, you will want to make the most of your specific training as you prepare your resume. The following will illustrate.

VOCATIONAL TRAINING HIGHLIGHTS   AUTO MECHANICS

Auto Mechanics Fundamentals
Building an Engine
Ignition Systems
Transmissions
Electrical Systems

Auto Service and Repair
Engine Removal
Engine Assembly
Tune-up, Engine Systems
Clutch Service

Automatic Transmission
Differential
Universal Joint Service

Air Conditioning Service

Brake Service

Next, if you had campus activities, honors or awards either academic or extra curricular, present them in your resume *if* they are pertinent or relevant to your objective. If they add to the word picture of *you*, include them; it's wise to limit the list to 4 or 5 items, and academic honors or campus-wide activities are best. For example, here are some typical listings.

STUDENT ACTIVITIES

Dean's List: 3 semesters
Grade Point Average last four quarters:
2.9/3.2/3.1/3.4 (Basis 4.0)
Graduated with High Honors

President, Student Senate
Chairman, Student Activities Committee
Secretary, Student Council
Representative, Student Advisory Council

Delta Kappa Epsilon - Social Fraternity: President; Vice President; Social Chairman; Pledge Trainer; Outstanding Pledge; Chairman, Mothers Weekend; Intramural Sports Chairman
Delta Phi Epsilon - Honorary International Trade and Foreign Service Fraternity: President

University International Emphasis Week: Publicity Chairman
Mock United Nations: Voting Delegate
Phi Delta Phi - Law School Social Fraternity: Historian

Church Activities
Reserve Officers Training Corps: Brigade Adjutant
Varsity Swimming Team

If your work experience includes any full time jobs, follow the suggestions given in Section II. Show your work experience in reverse chronological order. Let your summer work experience, if any, follow the full time work.

If you have summer work only, list it but avoid much detail, especially if the work was not related to your current objective. No need to spell out Responsibilities, and especially Achievements if they were non-existent or of a minor nature.

Keep in mind the principle of *not* overplaying whatever you did. In your summer work, it is usually not desirable to show earnings, and not necessary to show the reason for leaving each three-month job.

section 4

areas of knowledge/experience

Two different kinds of Check Lists are included in this Guide. The first, entitled "*Areas of Knowledge/Experience*" is useful in helping you to prepare correctly the "Areas of Knowledge and Experience" section on the first page of the Data Sheets. The second list, included in the next Section, headed "*Areas of Achievement*" is a tool for the preparation of the "Achievements" section of each page used in describing your current and past positions.

These Lists will help you to see what can be included in the two Areas, and how to make your own individual descriptive statements. They should not necessarily be copied word for word. They are designed to stimulate your thinking so that you can come up with your own important facts.

Consider first the "Areas of Knowledge/Experience" space on the first page of the Data Sheets. Use a Work Sheet and make a complete list of one or two word statements describing your knowledge gained from experience only. Do not include any educational areas in which you do not have some practical work experience.

Be honest and conservative. Be able to back up every statement you make. Include a maximum of 15 to 20 items. If your own experience can best be summed up in five phrases, then use just five. If you are a student without work experience, eliminate this section from your Resume.

The second of the "thought starter" check lists is headed "Areas of Achievement" and is useful in helping you to fill out the "Achievements" sections of each of the Data Sheets used in setting down your work history.

Study the "Areas of Achievement" check list not only to stimulate your thinking on *what* to list as your accomplishments, but *how* to list them. Be concise, but clear.

Remember: no long sentences, no long paragraphs.

INDEX

AREAS OF KNOWLEDGE/EXPERIENCE

Accounting/Controllership/Auditing

Controllership
General Accounting Administration
Policy Determination

General Accounting
Insurance Accounting
Brokerage Accounting
Financial Accounting
Industrial Accounting
Branch Accounting
Cost Accounting

Responsibility Accounting
  Cost Centers
  Profit Centers

Expense Control
Auditing
Accounting Systems

Inventory Control
Material Control

Payroll
Credit and Collection
Taxes
Insurance

Data Processing Usage
Computer Installation
Systems and Procedures

Departmental Administration
Office Management
Management Reporting
Records Retention

Public Accounting
Corporate Secretary
Financial Management
Investments
Financial Statements

Consolidations
Acquisitions, Dispositions

Capital Investments
Profit Planning
Tax Reduction

Budgets and Forecasts
Long Range Planning

Bank Relations

Financial Analysis
Financial Evaluation
Financial Projections

Cash Flow

Securities Portfolio
Real Estate Loans
Commercial Loans
Consumer Credit
Installment Lending
Leasing Programs

Acquisition Audits
Feasibility Studies

Personnel
Staff Supervision
Hiring
Training

Administrative Assistant

General Business Administration
Office Administration
  Office Services

Clerical Supervision

Credit and Collections
Accounts Receivable

Purchasing

Accounting
Cost Analysis
Finance

Sales
Sales Management
Sales Promotion

Advertising

Personnel
Employment
Traffic

Procedure Audits
Training
Data Processing
Systems and Procedures
Work Simplification
Work Flow
Work Measurement
Manual Preparation

Plant Management
Quality Control
Production Control

Public Relations
Publicity
Customer Relations

Supervision

Correspondence
Office Layout
Office Equipment

Administrative Office Services/Office Management

Office Administration
Staff Supervision
Departmental Administration

Office Layout and Construction
Office Equipment, Furniture
Office Moves
Lease Negotiation

Systems and Procedures
Forms and Methods
Work Measurement
Work Simplification
Work Flow
Procedure Audits

Manual Preparation

Expense Reduction

Office Services
  Mail, Filing
  Printing, Duplicating
  Stock—Supplies and Inventory
  Typing/Steno
  Switchboard
  Reception
  Maintenance

Statistics Analysis
Surveys

Salary Administration

Personnel
  Recruiting
  Testing
  Hiring
  Training
  Communications
  Employee Relations
  Fringe Benefits
  Credit Union

Purchasing

Credit
Accounting
Payroll
Insurance

Building Management

Customer Service
Order-Billing
Records

Security, Safety

Advertising

Advertising Agency Operation
Corporate Advertising Operations
Departmental Administration

Industrial Advertising
Consumer Advertising

Intangibles
Component Parts
Goods Consumed in Manufacture
Capital Equipment

Markets
    OEM, Commercial, Dealer, Service,
    Engineers, Contractors, etc.

Marketing Plan
Communications Objectives
Prospect Identification
Campaign Planning

Product Advertising
Corporate Advertising
Budgets
Media Analysis
Media Selection

Ad Creation
    Concept or Theme
    Illustrative Idea
    Layout
    Headline and Copy

Publication Advertising
Radio Advertising
TV Advertising

Direct Mail Campaigns
Response Analysis
Computer Use

Sales Promotion
Family Identification
Collateral Material
Sales Films
Training Films
Trade Shows
Exhibits/Displays
Hospitality Suites

Bulletins
Catalogs
Literature
Point-of-Purchase Material
Engineering and Technical
    Material
Installation and Service
    Material
Labeling
    (Sales, Technical, Legal)

House Magazine
Annual Reports

Merchandising Campaigns
Dealer Sales Aids
Dealer Incentive Programs

Tie-In Ads

Public Relations-Publicity
Trade Press

Air Industry

Aviation Industry
Commercial Pilot
Instrumentation
Flight Systems
Airplane Mechanics
Refueling Equipment

Flight Operations
Scheduling Rules
Union Contracts

Staff Liaison/Supervision
Personnel: Screening, Testing,
    Hiring
Employee Relations
Training Orientation

Customer Service
Sales
Public Contact
Complaint Handling

General Management
Operations Administration

Group and Charter Procedures
Air Freight Procedures

Personnel Scheduling
Quality Control
Cost Control
Space Control

Architecture

Architectural Design

Client Space Needs and Program
    Development
Site Selection, Analysis
Master Planning, Feasibility Studies

Interior Design
Equipment, Furnishings Selection
Contract Administration
Engineering Liaison

Project Management
Manpower Budgets, Scheduling

Cost Analysis, Estimating
Specification Writing
Building Code Analysis

Drafting
Sketching, Detailing
Federal Grant Applications

Projects
    Office, Commercial, Educational
        Buildings
    Arts and Sciences Building
    Shopping Center
    Hospital

Art/Illustrating

Art and Illustrating
    Pen and Ink
    Water Color
    Pencil
    Chalk
    Oil and Acrylic
    Tempera
    Wood Engraving
Photography
    Shooting
    Black & White Processing
    Tinting

Charts and Diagrams
Maps

Consumer Advertising
Ad Creation - Layout
Publication and TV Advertising
Collateral Material
Labels
House Organ

Package Design
Brochure Design

Artype
LeRoy Lettering

Associations

Association Management

Public Affairs
Government Affairs
    National, State
    County, Municipal

Trade Associations
Industrial Associations
Government Commissions

Government Relations
Industrial Relations
Public Relations
Community Relations
Labor Relations

Business Conference Development
Convention Planning, Management

Legislation
  Bill Drafting
  Lobbying
  Representation to:
    Legislative Bodies,
    Departments, Bureaus,
    Commissions
Research and Reporting
  Writing
  Publications
  Speaking
Financing, Budgets
Expense Control
Membership Development
Personnel, Employment
Staff Supervision

Automotive
Factory/Dealer Policies
  and Procedures
Owner Relations
Service Management
Departmental Administration
Service Expense, Budgets
Work Scheduling
Tracing, Expediting
Parts Control, Management
Complete Maintenance and Service
Supervision of Employees
Training
Personal Productive Effort
  Master Mechanic
Product Knowledge
Mechanical Knowledge
Diagnostic Skills
Customer Sales
Complaint Handling
Customer Correspondence
Diesel Specialist
Liaison:
  Vendor Representatives
  Manufacturers Reprs.
  Customers
  Parent Company
Financing
Insurance

Banking
Senior Administration
Operations Management

Finance
Financial Analysis
Directors Reports
Operating Budgets
Securities Investment
Trust Operations
Commercial Loans
Real Estate Loans
Accounts Administration
Business Development
Business Acquisitions
Installment Lending
  Autos
  Mobile Homes
  Appliances, Furniture
  Direct Loans
  Auto Leasing
Controllership
Auditing, Internal
Systems and Methods
Data Processing Applications
Teller Operations
Bookkeeping
Customer/Dealer Relations

Brokerage/Securities/Intangibles
Stocks
Corporate Bonds
Municipal Bonds
Mutual Funds
Government Securities
Cash Grain Merchandising
Commodity Futures Trading
Grain Inspection
General Commodity Inspection
Exchange Floor Operation
Marketing Programs
Sales Direction
Money Management
Chart Analysis
Compliance
OTC Trading
General Management
Division Management
Branch Management
Sales Management
High Volume Selling
Major Account Contact
Institutional Sales
Administration: Operations,
  Compliance, Sales

Recruitment: Hiring, Training,
  Supervision
Client Relations
Business and Financial
  Community Relations

Clubs/Restaurants/Hotels
Hotel Operations
Administrative Housekeeping
Work Planning, Scheduling
Personnel Allocation
Hiring, Training
Supervision, Inspection
Union Relations
Inventory Control
Purchasing
Catering and Restaurant Manageme
Personal Hospitality
Menu Planning, Sales
Food and Beverage Preparation
  and Service
Entertainment
Dining Rooms, Bar, Banquet
Private Meeting Rooms
Conventions
Outside Parties
Kitchen Facilities
Kitchen Equipment
Plate Service
Buffet Service
Cold Buffet
Bakery
Customer Relations
Public Relations
Budgets
Specialty Restaurant Business
General Hotel Management
Office Administration
Maintenance
Front Desk Operations
Reservations
Credit approval
Hotel Audit

Construction/Contracting
Construction Management
Contract Administration
Subcontract Agreements
Bidding
Estimating: Takeoffs, Changes
Cost Analysis, Forecasts, Control

Contract Terminations
Supervision
Contract Payouts
Coordination Meetings
Expediting: Fabrication, Assembly,
  Delivery
Progress Schedules, CPM
Blue Prints, Shop Drawings
Change Orders
Purchasing Supplies
Correspondence
Site Selection
Land Development
Office Services Management
General Business Administration
Community Relations
Property Management
Residential Sales
Apartment Sales
Commercial Real Estate
Income Property
Financing
Purchasing
Mortgaging
Real Estate Taxes
General Construction
  Institutional
  Residential
  Light Commercial

Consulting

Business Planning
Business Administration
Corporate Development
  and Appraisal
Management Surveys
Management Analysis
Management Engineering
Operations Analysis and Research
Business Measurements
Forecasting
  Labor, Market, Expense
Systems and Procedures
Computer Programming
Equipment Utilization
General Administration
Policy Determination
Operating Management
Sales Management
Research and Development
Management Communications
Executive Training

Manufacturing
  Programming
  Systems and Technology
  Problem Analysis
  Solution Techniques
Transportation: All Modes
Distribution
Finance Management
Employee/Labor Relations

Credit

Credit Management
Collections
Credit Investigation
Departmental Administration
Accounts Receivable
Industrial
Consumer
Sales Financing
Wholesale
Retail
Financial Analysis
Financial Projections
Customer/Dealer Relations
Branch Credit
Office Administration
Systems and Procedures
Budgets
Data Processing Usage
Attorney Relations
Collection Agencies
Staff Supervision
Hiring
Training

Customer Service

Service Training Instruction
Service Management
Customer Sales
Customer Orders
Expediting and Tracing
Complaints
Liaison with Sales Representatives
Liaison with Manufacturers
  Representatives
Liaison with Customers
Liaison with Manufacturing
Customer Correspondence
Telephone Inquiries
Telephone Sales

Data Processing

Data Processing Management
Staff Supervision
Departmental Coordination
Systems Design
T. P. Systems
Teleprocessing
Operations Research
Feasibility Studies
Hardware Evaluation
Methods and Procedures
Software Development
Systems Programming
Data Administration
Computer Installations
Computer Conversions
Programming
Tape-Disk-Data Cell-Drum
Virtual Core Storage
Applications for:
  Accounting
  Accounts Payable
  Accounts Receivable
  Payroll
  Sales
  Sales Analysis
  Orders
  Traffic
  Purchasing
  Personnel
  Collections
  Customer Information Control
    Systems
  Freight Rates
  Warehousing
  Production Control, Inventory,
    and Distribution
  Insurance: Life, Group,
    and Casualty
  Hospital Information Systems and
    Biomedical Applications
  Management Information Control
    Systems
  Feasibility and Implementation
    Studies
  Hardware and Software Evaluation
    Studies
Hardware:
  IBM—360/20, 30, 40, 50, 65, 370
    series, System/3
  RCA—Spectra 70/35, 45
  Honeywell—316, 516, 632, H-1648
    Time Sharing System, H-200
  CDC—1700, 3100, 3150, 3300,
    3500, 6400, 6500, 6600, 7600
  Burroughs—2500, 3500, 5500

Peripheral Hardware:
    Cards, papertape, magnetic tapes, drums, disks and large fixed disks, data cells, CRT's.

Languages:
    Fortran
    Cobol
    ANS Cobol
    RPG
    PL1
    BAL
    Compass
    O/S JCL

Operating Systems:
    IBM—DOS, TOS, DOS-COS, O/S-MVT and MFT.
    CDC—Master, MSOS, AFPAM, MEDLAB, SCOPE
    Burroughs—MCP

Designing

Machine Design
Machine Drafting and Detailing
Mechanical Design and Drafting
Architectural Drafting and Detailing

Industrial Product Development
    Materials: Metal, Plastics, Wood

Interiors—Conceptual/
    Environmental Design of Homes
        Condominiums
        Apartments
        Showrooms
        Offices

Arch./Eng. Coordination
Finishes Presentation
Furniture Presentation
Cost Estimating
Space Planning

Working Drawings
Shop Drawings
Millwork Details
Color Selection
Contract Documents

Product Development
Photography
Illustration and Rendering
Drafting

Client Contact
Customer Education

Education

Business School Administration
    Staff Supervision
    Personnel, Training

School Administration
    Instructional Supervision
    Student Conduct and Discipline
    School Patrol
    Proposal Development and Writing
        (Federal and State Funds)
    Psychological Testing
    Pupil Personnel Services
    Financial Administration
    Costs and Budgets
    Activity Programming
    Curriculum Development

Teaching
    Pre-School, Grade School, Junior
        High School, High School
    Special Education
    Departmental—Language Arts,
        Mathematics, Social Studies,
        Science, Art, Guidance, etc.
    Team Teaching
    Accelerated Groups
    Remedial Groups
    Open Classroom

Counseling

Student Leadership
Team Coaching
Student Supervision

Faculty Relations
Parent-Teacher Relations

Engineering - Chemical/Metallurgical

Chemical Engineering
Project Engineering
Design Drafting

Metallurgical Engineering
Metallurgical Research

Materials Engineering

New Process Planning
New Process Development
Fabricating Process Techniques
Refractory Metals
Alloy Development

Materials Testing
Testing Equipment
Measurement Techniques
    and Instruments

Spectrographic Analyses
Ultrasonic Applications
Stress Corrosion
Processing Lubricants
Metal/Chemical Problems

Engineering - Design

Production Machinery Design
Product Design
Packaging

Tool Design
Die and Mold

Time/Cost Quotations
Design Consultation
Departmental Liaison
Shop Scheduling
Staff Supervision
Model Shop

Engineering - Electrical

Electrical Engineering
Electro-Mechanical Engineering

Project Engineering
Project Supervision

Application Engineering
Power Distribution

Lighting
Lighting Standards
Electrical Design Drafting

Control Circuit Test Sets
Alternator
Electrical Measuring Instruments
Timing Circuits
Semiconductor Devices

Variable Voltage Control
A. C. Motor Control
A. C. Control Relaying
Solid State Control
Numerical Controlled Machine
    Circuits

Industrial Computer Control
Remote Control Equipment

Design of Experiments
Systems Design/Development
Selection and Rating of Componen
Data Processing Usage

Staff Supervision
Hiring, Training

Engineering - Electronics

Electronics Engineering
Control Electronics

Audio Systems
High Fidelity
Electro-Mechanical Systems
Project Engineering

Research and Development
Scientific Instrumentation
Basic, Theoretical and Applied
   Research
New Product Development
Prototype Fabrication
Electronic Test Equipment

Production Engineering
Production Startup
Electronics Maintenance

Tooling Design
Numerical Controls

Communications

Staff Supervision

Departmental Liaison

Computer Usage

Engineering - Industrial

Industrial Engineering
Project Engineering
Long Range Planning
Production Management

Inventory Control
Cost Control

Material Handling and Storage

Maintenance Systems

Economic Analysis
Distribution Analysis

Facilities Planning and Construction

Work Measurement
Time Standards

CPM, PERT
Computer Usage

Staff Supervision
Hiring, Training

Engineering - Maintenance

Maintenance Management

Engineering Maintenance
Preventive Maintenance
Maintenance Supervision

Purchasing
Budgets and Forecasts
Cost Control

Building Construction

Union Negotiations
Performance Reviews
Salary Administration

Staff Supervision

Data Processing

Engineering - Mechanical

Engineering Administration
Mechanical Engineering
Project Engineering
Production Engineering
Production Control

Systems Design & Development
   Thermodynamics Systems
   Environmental Control Systems
   Linear Control Systems
   Aircraft Fuel Systems

Test Engineering
Test Equipment Design
R & D Projects

Application Engineering
Feasibility Testing
Machinery—Design, Engineering
Production Startup
Preventive Maintenance

Purchased Product Testing
Product Modification
Computer Usage

Departmental Supervision
   Technicians
   Draftsmen
   Lab Personnel

Contractor Collaboration

Staff Supervision

Engineering - Project

Construction
Mechanical
Electrical
Electro-Mechanical
Civil
Maintenance
Machinery
Fixtures

Design
Field Surveys
Installation
Startup

Field Supervision

Specifications Development
Vendor Selection
Purchasing
Supplier Contracts

MTM
CPM
PERT

Data Processing Usage

**Engineering - Research
and Development**

Design
Specifications

Projections
Forecasts, Budgets
Negotiations, Contracts

Appropriation Engineering
Electrical Engineering
Mechanical Engineering
Industrial Engineering
Project Engineering

Research and Development
Feasibility Studies
Testing and Evaluation

Quality Control
Packaging

Technical Management
Technical Sales
Consulting

Facilities Planning
Machinery Design

Statistical Analysis

Administrative Management
Departmental Liaison
Staff Supervision
Training

Computer Usage
CPM
PERT
Value Analysis

Finance

Securities
Investments
Profit Planning
Expense Reduction

Financial Projections
Management Reporting
Operations Analysis
Long-Range Planning
Feasibility Studies

Banking
Trust Operations
Operations Management

Retail Investments Evaluation:
   Sales Finance, Direct Loan
Floor Planning
Financial Statement Analysis
Auditing for Compliance

Program Development:
  Operations, Marketing
Facility: Site Selection,
  Lease Administration
State Banking Liaison
Expense Budgeting
Attorney Relations

Financial Analysis

Financial Analysis
Financial Projections
Acquisition and Feasibility Studies
Profit Planning
Capital Investment
Long Range Planning

Budgets
Tax Reductions
Expense Reductions

Policy Formulation
Management Reporting
Banking

Business Administration
Systems and Procedures
Accounting, Auditing

Market Research
Market Potential Evaluation
Supervision

General Management

General Management
Organizational Structure
Policy Determination
Operating Procedures

Acquisitions
Dispositions

Marketing
Advertising
Merchandising
Product Line Development
Pricing and Margins

Cost Control

Trade Relations
Public Relations
Customer Relations
Employee-Labor Relations

Finance
Cash Flow

Budgets, Forecasts

Sales Management
Manufacturing-Production
Purchasing
Distribution

Hospital/Nursing Center/Medical

Hospital Administration
Nursing Center Administration

Nursing Care
Diet Preparation
Medical Liaison
Paramedic Work

Accounting and Finance
Budgets
Inventory and Supply
Purchasing

Medical Planning
Disaster Planning

Personnel Administration
  Examination Development
  Testing, Training

Service Department Control
  Housekeeping
  Laundry
  Food Service
  Plant Operation
  Plant Maintenance
  Security, Safety

Complaint Investigation
  Medical, Accident
Public Relations

Insurance

Life: Group, Individual

Accident and Health
Hospitalization
Major Medical
Disability

Home Owners
Automobile
Property
Marine

Fire and Theft

Travel Accident

Pensions
Employee Benefits
Credit Life

Sales
Sales Management

Territory Coverage

Quotas

Inventory Control

Inventory Control
Material Control
Production Control
Material Systems and Procedure
Value Analysis

Material Handling and Storage
Warehouse Layout
Plant/Warehouse Management
Order Production

Traffic
  Motor
  Freight
  Steamship

Numerically Controlled Equipment

Purchasing Management
Purchasing Policy
  Development
Production Purchasing

Vendor Evaluation, Relations
Expediting
Contract Preparation

Data Processing Applications

Reporting Controls
Shipping
Receiving

Line Supervision
Hiring, Training

Legal

General Practice
Corporate Law
Patent Law
Educational Law

Criminal Law
Banking Law
Real Estate Law
Commercial Lending

Patent Applications
Licensing Agreements
Trademarks
Antitrust
Contracts
Leases

Wills
Trusts
Taxes

Purchase Agreements
Sales Agreements

Securities Registration

Corporate Organization
Capital Structure

Legal Research
Evidence
Trial Practice
Appeals

Labor Relations
Negotiations
Arbitration

Library

Personnel Administration
Budget Planning and Control
Building Location, Layout

Adult Book Selection
Work Simplification
Training Workshops

Library Board Liaison
Community Activities
Customer Relations

Report Preparation
News Bulletins
Publicity

Marketing

Marketing
Market Plan Formats
Forecasts—1 year, 5 year
Performance Appraisal Programs

Departmental Administration
Organizational Structure
Policy Determination

Sales Promotion
Sales Meetings
Demonstrations
Trade Shows

Advertising Management

Sales Management
Sales Training and Supervision

Market Research
Trend Analysis
Media Evaluation
Survey Design
Market Potential Evaluation

Budgeting

Distribution

OEM Accounts
Proprietary Accounts

Premium Sales
Catalog Sales
Contract Sales
Government Sales

Brand Management
Product Management
Product Line Development

Merchandising
Packaging
Pricing

Wholesale
Retail

Distributors
Dealers
Manufacturers Agents

Application Engineering
Sales Engineering
Design Engineering

Personnel/Industrial Relations/Labor Relations

Personnel Policies
  Formulation
  Writing
  Administration
  Communication

Benefits Administration
  Insurances
  Pensions
  Profit Sharing
  Stock Purchases
  Vacations, Holidays

Salary Administration
  Job Descriptions
  Job Classifications
  Job Evaluation
  Rate Ranges
  Progression

Recruitment and Employment
  Executive, Administrative
  Professional
  Sales
  Plant
  Clerical

Hiring—testing, screening, selecting

Employee Relations
Training
Orientation
Counseling
Employee Communications

Personnel Procedures and Forms
  Development, Implementation

Turnover Control

Records Maintenance

Department Administration

Budget Control

Industrial Relations
Labor Relations
Labor Negotiations

Union Relationships
Arbitration
Grievances
Union Contracts

Labor Law
  Case Preparation
  Trial Practice

Labor Relations Policies
National Mediation Board
National Labor Relations Board
Industrial Relations Seminars

Plant Management

Plant Management

Industrial Engineering

Manufacturing Engineering
Production Methods
Product Line Design
Proficiency Techniques

Production Standards

Operations Administration

Production Control
Projections
Scheduling

Purchasing

Inventory Control

Materials Control

Loss and Scrap Control

Industrial Relations
Labor Relations
Union Negotiations
Personnel

Manpower Allocation
Compensation Plans
Rates
Time and Motion Studies
Wage Incentive Systems

Cost Calculations
Estimating

Budgeting

Quality Control
Specification Production

Programming Product Formulation

Government Contracts

Systems and Procedures
Data Processing Applications

Staff Supervision
Hiring, Training

Police/Law Enforcement/Security

Law/Security

Administration
Operations
Investigative Expertise
Report Writing

Supervision of Detectives
Training Supervision
Communications Administration
Departmental Instruction

Budget Preparation
Files Maintenance
Investigation Assignments

Teaching, Seminars
Research
Academic Program Planning
Curriculum Development

Crime Detection
Crime Patterns
Apprehend Criminals

Criminal Complaints
Search Warrants
Arrests
Case Coordination

State Statutes

Consultant on Police Matters
Internal Investigations Experience

Line and Staff Supervision
Testing, Hiring, Training
Rating and Selection for Promotion

Production Control

Production Control
Inventory Control
Materials Control
Production Scheduling

Systems and Procedures
Forms and Report Design
Feasibility Studies

PERT
Line of Balance
E.O.Q.
R.O.P.

Inspection
Expediting

Data Processing Applications

Reporting Controls
  Purchasing Forecasts
    and Performance
  Manufacturing
  Production Changes
  Engineering Changes
  Contract Completion
  Loss and Scrap

Shipping
Receiving
Tool Crib
Timekeeping

Line Supervision
Hiring
Training

Public Relations

Public Relations
Fund Raising

Customer Relations

Sales
Convention Planning
Trade Shows, Displays
Demonstrator Promotions

Educational Programs
Market Surveys

Proposal Writing
Speech Writing
News Releases
Meeting Arrangements

Brochures

Feature Writing
Research

Office Administration
Liaison and Coordination

Purchasing

Purchasing Management
Departmental Administration
Purchasing Policy Development
Purchasing Systems and Procedures

Vendor Evaluation, Selection
Vendor Relations

Expediting
Coordinating
Problem Solving

Inventory Control
Material Handling, Storage

Product Analysis
Materials Changes

Negotiation
Contracts
Open End Ordering

Purchasing Quantity Control
Purchasing Timing Control

Staff Supervision
Employment, Training
Computer Usage

Real Estate

Real Estate
  Evaluations, Acquisitions
  Administration, Dispositions

Negotiations

Market Analysis

Site Criteria, Analysis
  Selection, Improvement

Options, Leases, Mortgages
Construction
Financing
Project Development

Franchising
Contractual Management
Property Administration

Contract Law
Legal Documentation

Profit Responsibility

Leasing
Repairs and Maintenance Control

Advertising Plans
Promotional Supervision

Appraisal
  Residential
  Commercial
  Vacant Land

Sales and Brokerage

Loan Underwriting
Foreclosures

Mortgage Financing

Feasibility Studies

Union Contract Negotiation
Employee-Labor Relations

Rental Rates Establishment
Rental Collections
Owner Statements Approval
Tenant Service, Complaints

Sales/Sales Management

Sales Administration

Personal Selling of Key Accounts
National Account Contact

Recruiting and Hiring
Sales Training
Sales Supervision

Territory Layout
Compensation Plans
Quota Development

Sales Forecasting
Budgeting—Expense and Sales
Expense Control

Specification Sales
Contract Sales
Lease Contracts
Government Contracts
Premium Sales

Sales Promotions, Contests
Advertising
Sales Aids, Kits, etc.

Customer Relations
Displays
Trade Shows
Demonstrations
Marketing
Merchandising
Pricing
Packaging
Distribution Patterns
Brand Management
Product Management
Product Line Development
Wholesale
Retail
Industry
OEM
Manufacturers Representative
Dealers—Set-up
Distributors—Control
Contractors
Sub-contractors
Architects
Engineers
Applicators

Social Work
Teaching
Tutoring
Program Development
Public Relations
Written Communications
Public Speaking
Staff Supervision
Performance Evaluation
Departmental Liaison
Office Administration
Vocational Counseling
Personnel Training

Systems
Systems Administration
Departmental Management
Staff Supervision
Systems Analysis and Coordination
Applications for:
  Billing, Orders
  Accounts Payable
  Accounts Receivable
  Record Storage and Retrieval

Statistical Analysis
Payroll
Accounting, Sales
Production, Inventory
Traffic, Purchasing
Personnel
Operations Research
Feasibility Studies
Methods
Data Processing
Computer Installations
Computer Conversion
Programming
  1401
  360/20
  360/30
  360/70
  Honeywell
  Tape
  Disc
  Data Cell

Traffic
Traffic Administration
  Transportation
Distribution
Warehousing
Inventory Control
Site Selection: Plants, Bulk
  Terminals, Warehouses
Transportation Patterns
Routing, Tracing, Expediting
Freight Classification Changes
Rates—Information and Adjustments
Equalization Rates
Commodity Rate Establishment
Loss and Damage Claims
Loss and Damage—Preventive
  Research
Travel Arrangements
Fleet Car Administration
Garage Administration
Trucking
Equipment—Rail, Truck, Water
Shipping and Receiving
Dispatching
Materials Handling
Materials Handling Equipment
Packaging and Containers
  Specifications, Research,
  Permit-testing

Equipment Utilization Standards
Employee Productivity Standards
Research: Rates, Services, Methods
ICC Practice
Federal Transportation Laws
State Transportation Laws
Leases and Charters
Budgeting
Union Negotiation
Procedure Writing and
  Implementation
Traffic Information: Dissemination
  and Interpretation

Warehousing
Warehouse Management
Handling of Key National Accounts
Distribution Centers
Warehousing Facilities and Practices
Site Selection
Materials Handling
Materials Handling Equipment
Inventory Control
Loss and Damage Claims
Trucking
Routing, Tracing, Expediting
Rates
Lease Contracts
Expense Controls
Office Management
Staff Supervision
Payroll
Sanitation Controls
Sales
Advertising
Pricing
Computer Usage
Liaison with:
  Labor Unions
  Corporate Attorneys
  Construction Engineers
  Contractors

section 5

areas of achievement

INDEX

AREAS OF ACHIEVEMENT

Accounting, Controllership, Auditing

Improved closing date time from 10 working days to 7.

Speeded up billing cycle and increased cash flow by $150,000.

Lowered fees of outside CPA firm from $20,000 to $13,000 per year with internal control reviews quarterly.

Set up ABC inventory control system; lowered inventory $1 million annually and increased turnover from 3x to 5x.

Saved $10,000 annually in Accounting Department operating costs by rearranging workloads and removing unproductive personnel.

Developed and successfully administered a full budget program, with responsibility centers.

Designed and installed an effective budget forecasting and reporting system.

Reduced accounts receivable by over $30,000, with improved credit and collection policies.

Reduced inventory by $200,000 through analysis of turnover, production and handling.

Increased corporate blanket insurance coverage by $20 million, with additional premium cost of only $5,000.

Reduced annual recurring expenses $100,000 through work simplification, control procedures and staff reduction.

Saved $20,000 yearly through application of data processing to costs and budgets.

Improved cash flow forecasting.

Developed a scrap reporting system for a large defense manufacturer.

Instituted an inventory reduction program for a major publishing firm.

Produced faster and better financial and statistical data by converting machine accounting to data processing.

Participated substantially in the design and implementation of cost reduction program which saved $75,000 annually.

Increased profits 10% by revising price structure to reasonably reflect total cost and profit.

Successfully organized internal audit functions to handle coordinated financial and operational audits in diversified corporate activities in the U.S. and abroad.

Standardized the public accounting scope and performance of worldwide audits.

Produced thousands of dollars for the State of Illinois through careful examinations.

Administrative Assistant

Handled planning, layout and supervision of major office move, involving 20,000 square feet of space.

Reduced filing costs and errors substantially by replacing alpha system with terminal digit plan.

Saved $10,000 annually by reducing overall cost of outside purchases through supplier bid analyses.

Successfully worked with all levels of management to obtain final approval for new work-flow system.

As Administrative Assistant to the President, supervised the daily functioning of his four personal offices.

In the absence of the President, responsible for delegating the handling of all his mail to other executives, his secretaries or handling it personally.

Hosted and attended Company affairs and dinners; received dignitaries, business associates, government officials and personal friends of the President, and acted as host in his behalf.

Administrative Office Services / Office Management

Remodeled mailroom; increased efficiencies permitted staff reduction from 16 to 13 employees.

Successfully established and integrated in one new department all office services functions of 4 separate Divisions.

Initiated a formal, effective records retention program.

Cost justified purchase of $58,000 in new duplicating equipment, which improved quality and provided substantial cost savings.

Successfully relocated a corporate office of 130 people exactly on schedule, with no loss of effectiveness, over one weekend.

Developed and implemented an in-plant printing shop from inception to a 10-man department doing $250,000 per year.

Saved $5,000 annually by changing supplier of stationery and stocking by vendor; improved delivery time substantially.

Effected an $8,000 savings with telephone controls plus more efficient PBX operations.

Decreased office supply expense by 10%, through forms improvement and inventory control.

Successfully coordinated customer service, parts and sales with office functions.

Set up position descriptions and standards of performance for all office positions.

Increased office production totals in spite of 20% decrease in staff.

Advertising

Planned and implemented effective advertising, public relations, and dealer incentive programs.

Through market analysis and questionnaires identified *prime* prospects—greatly increasing productivity of subsequent ads.

Profitably switched ads from marginal-result publications to significantly productive ones.

Developed and implemented a successful overall Communications Plan based on marketing objectives.

Created ads that were directly responsible for leads that produced $100,000 in additional sales volume.

Accomplished substantial *increases* in ad readership, awareness of company and products, inquiry level, sales aids, market information.

Air Industry

Successfully built a Reservations Office, with 75% new employees into an effective operating unit in less than 3 months.

Effected an average monthly savings of over $2,500 by realigning Bell Telephone System lines.

Because of broad knowledge of the industry, Company, and procedures, was assigned to "trouble shoot" any department in need of attention; reorganized the problem departments.

Pilot Qualifications: private pilot; commercial pilot; flight instructor (airplane and instruments; multi-engine rating; instrument rating)

Air Medal with 31 Oak Leaf Clusters, Bronze Star Medal.

Knowledgeable in aircraft systems, Company policies, and Federal Aviation Administration regulations.

Architecture

Successfully managed projects under budgets, with an overall resulting 12%-15% profitability.

Managed projects, developed building programs, master plans, and feasibility studies for over $52 million construction.

Completed suburban high school project construction documents for $13 million in record 5 months.

Introduced innovative techniques in nursing home administrative area to allow for future growth.

Successfully developed and was responsible for over 90 educational and commercial projects exceeding $48 million in construction cost.

Successfully completed first contemporary $5 million city hall in ultraconservative voting district.

Projects and Services:
    Health Care Facilities—Nursing Homes, Clinics
    Public Schools
    Offices
    Banks
    Community Theater
    Governmental Buildings
    Commercial Buildings
    Industrial Buildings
    Recreational Buildings

    University of Illinois, Chicago—Union Building
    Carthage College, Kenosha, Wisconsin
    Carson Pirie Scott and Company, Chicago—Restaurant
    Woodmar Shopping Center, Hammond, Indiana

Art/Illustrating

Illustrations have been published in approximately 40 textbooks, encyclopedias, or scientific volumes at the college level.

Have 2 paintings on exhibit at LaSalle County Historical Museum, Utica, Illinois.

Prepared work for major companies: Firestone Tires; International Harvester; Sargent and Fisher.

Prepared brochures, personally doing the illustrating and art work, photography, copy and lay-outs.

Established a good degree of harmony and coordination between the Art Department and Production.

Award winner in show of national scope. Additional awards at local and regional shows.

Associations

Took significant action on 70-85 legislative bills each session.

Was successful in 95% of the attempts throughout the years.

Saved the business community over $500,000 by defeating adverse bills.

Established a productive working arrangement between Industry and Municipal Government.

Authored successful state legislation on many measures, including air pollution, industry defense, wage assignments and garnishments.

Wrote numerous Department reports on Congressional bills which were approved to submit to Committee chairmen.

Drafted statement of Chamber witness before Senate Labor subcommittee on wage-hour legislation.

Wrote numerous Chamber pamphlets on legislative issues.

Built membership rolls by 10% net each year for 5 consecutive years.

Automotive

Increased service sales by 35% within 3 months.

Reduced customer service complaints.

Established a new price schedule for repairs.

Reduced lost time on repair work by 50%.

Established a solid training program for apprentices.

Personally handled all warranty claims; result was a 90% return of all credit for which applied.

Set up good maintenance program for fleet customers.

Established an excellent repair service relationship with customers; trained 2 mechanics on diesel engine repairs.

Saved $10,000 annually by doing all truck painting on the premises.

Started as a mechanic and became Assistant Service Manager in 3½ years.

Banking

Successfully managed the Department; operated at above average profit.

Handled outstandings of $4 million in commercial and $4 million in retail installment loans with a staff of 2 officers and 6 employees.

Reduced bad debt write-offs from 2% to .5%.

Recovered $15,000 previously written off without use of collection agency.

Established good liaison with Sales Department and reduced total number of poor risk accounts.

Instigated plan in Bank of shorting treasury bills in excess of $6 million to reduce federal funds borrowings; saved over $100,000 in interest cost.

Initiated and/or implemented loans totalling up to $250,000.

Originated new demand deposits of over $700,000.

Introduced new savings accounts of over $100,000.

Bank achieved a growth rate of $2.5 million per year.

In 15 months, built retail outstanding from $5 million to $22 million; increased wholesale outstanding from $1 million to $7 million.

Built the Branch from a position of no loans and no customers at the opening to profitability 3 years ahead of projections.

Brokerage/Securities/Intangibles

Built the Midwestern Division to No. 1 ranking in production and profit for the entire company.

Developed a retail clientele, with gross production exceeding 6 figures in first 18 months.

Personal trading position showed a profit every year ranging from a low of 20% to a high of 40%.

Started as a back office clerk, progressed to sales and the realization of a personal target of $100,000 plus gross production.

Established an effective day-to-day communication between the USDA Grain Market Reporter and the Commodity Exchange Authority.

Developed investment proposal for venture capital for a new firm in an energy-related field.

Reduced total operations staff at Branches 10% by work measurement studies; saved $90,000 per year.

Opened over 200 accounts in 2½ years as a Registered Representative.

Coordinated Company presentation to State of Idaho for management of $100,000 million in State funds.

Clubs/Restaurants/Hotels

Increased food and beverage sales by 15% in 6 months.

Reduced annual operating costs 12% the first year.

Handled all expenditures within budgetary limits.

Reduced labor costs through better work scheduling.

Acquired great success through personal attention to every detail involved in handling parties/conventions and acting as personal host.

Built satisfied customers, including major companies.

Greatly increased sales of food and beverage at the resort through ability to sell higher priced menus.

Saved up to 30% per year in food costs by controls over receiving, spoilage and inventories.

Through improved selection, training, and supervision, upgraded the quality and performance of the restaurant personnel.

Improved beverage service for 2 restaurants and room service through design and construction supervision of new service bar.

Improved hotel security through close supervision and scheduling.

Initiated written procedures and trained the staff in service for catered parties in the major entertainment room.

Construction/Contracting

Successfully maintained construction progress per schedule.

Handled liaison contacts with engineering companies and governmental agencies for acquisition of new business.

Designed and built these structures in Chicago:

1606 W. Catalpa Street	94 apartments
5910 N. Kenmore Avenue	65 apartments
3604 Pinegrove	60 apartments
Factory building, Rockwell St.	75,000 sq. feet

Increased rent volume 15% on new construction.

Constructed over 150 custom-built homes, ranging in value to $90,000.

Completed a wide range of buildings including churches, industrial, commercial and others:

Redeemer Lutheran Church, South Holland, Illinois
Calumet Park Municipal Swimming Pool, Calumet Park, Illinois
Frito-Lay Company—Warehouse, Lansing, Illinois

Completed a multi-million dollar project on schedule and within budget to the satisfaction of the U.S. Government.

Consulting

Reduced a bank payroll by 36%, improved customer service.

Reduced steel fabrication downtime by 32%, rejects by 14%.

Reduced labor costs substantially in an 1800-bed hospital.

Increased sales 23% for distributor, without increasing salesmen or hours.

Designed and installed an operating control system for a meat packer which resulted in a 46% increase in pounds per employee hour.

Work done for a paper company accommodated a tight timetable on a new coater installation; client satisfaction opened up extensive new assignments.

Engineered a new plant layout, calculated burden rates, established breakeven charts.

Eliminated substantial losses permitting company to survive; reduced inventory $250,000, cut salaries by $100,000.

Saved $26,000 annually by revamping tooling on one model; saved $48,000 by retooling another model.

Credit

Reduced bad debt writeoffs from 2% to less than ½ of 1%.

Lowered turnover from 48 days to 36.4 days.

Recovered $5,600 previously written off, without use of collection agencies.

Reduced total Credit Department staff by 4 people, through consolidating divisional credit operations.

Built good customer relations while reducing total accounts receivable by $30,000.

Established effective liaison with Sales Department and reduced total number of poor risk accounts.

Installed new system for cash application; set up a training program.

Reorganized the reporting process and improved report form.

Successful in building and maintaining excellent customer relations; solved numerous credit problems and retained both customer goodwill and the sales volume.

Set up a control procedure to automatically review and investigate "over 30-day" delinquent accounts.

Customer Service

Speeded handling of quality complaints from 2-3 weeks to 1 week; service complaint handling from 1-2 weeks to 3 days.

Established a staff training program covering internal procedures, outside traffic and warehousing services, and Company products and usages; entire inside staff better able to handle customer sales, service and technical needs.

Reduced customer order complaints by 18% in one year by setting up new control and follow-up system for order handling.

Reduced the typing lag on call reports and memos from 7-10 days to 3 days.

Initiated a successful service complaint preventive program; saved $500 a month locally on demurrage, adjustments and freight charges, and was adopted by the Company nationally and saved $2,000 a month.

Established pre-season inventories of parts, reducing repair time from 2-3 week industry norm to 5 days.

Data Processing

Saved $10,000 annually in Accounting Department alone through computer systems applications for payroll, budgets, and receivables/payables.

Reduced monthly computer time for Accounts Payable/Accounts Receivable from 25 hours to 15 hours through newly upgraded accounting systems.

Developed and installed Data Processing applications:

Sales Statistics	General Accounting	Scheduling
Forecasting	Finance	Expediting
Budgeting	Payroll	Inventory Control
Cost Controls	Production	Accounts Payable
	Order/Billing	Accounts Receivable

Successfully converted
Manual systems to computerized automation systems
Tape systems to disk-oriented systems
DOS systems to 360/70 systems

Successfully installed nationwide teleprocessing systems.

Made successful and timely conversion of all systems from a medium scale Honeywell disk/tape/data communication facility to a Burroughs B-3500.

Revamped and made workable a library of 300 programs comprising 25 distinct application areas inherited from previous staff.

Implemented an on-line/real time utility billing system to eliminate a $150,000 backlog of unbilled services.

Designing

Successfully completed color selection for furniture and equipment for 3 Chicago public schools; handled installation in one school.

Designed and developed a trade exhibit used successfully nationwide.

Final design solutions for a condominium were shown in a national shelter magazine.

Successfully established a creative in-house design department which produced high acceptance by Sears.

Designed a number of plastic frames which became basic, high sales items.

Designed a highly successful console for a computerized type composing unit.

Assisted in completion of two new models ready for production.

Prepared a complete set of working drawings for ABC Company remodeling 2 floors.

Education

Successfully implemented an involved progressive program of team teaching and non-graded student rating.

Initiated, satisfactorily, a new philosophy for discipline problems.

Implemented a program for the educationally gifted child.

Installed a foreign language laboratory.

Began a program to individualize instruction.

Introduced a special program for a minority group.

Established exceptional rapport with primary level children; maintained good personal relations with parents, faculty and staff.

Raised the reading level of the primary children; successfully guided the children in handling increased responsibilities.

Conducted a successful 8th Grade graduation program and party.

Led the girls' Softball Team to 2nd place in the league.

Assisted Safety Patrol members in earning awards for outstanding service.

Created a successful in-service training program in data processing and computer programming for public and parochial school teachers.

Established very productive placement, industrial and high school programs.

Produced and directed a 30-minute television program for WFLD-TV, Channel 32.

Engineering - Chemical / Metallurgical

Initiated technological changes that reduced manpower requirements, doubled plant output, reduced raw material inventory and cut overall costs by 15%.

Developed potentially patentable lubricant for improved drawing of electron beam melted tantalum tubing.

Assisted in the development of the first successful process for producing continuous lengths of tantalum sheets converting ingot to final product.

Developed a salt bath annealing facility resulting in low initial cost, low unit cost and high output.

Participated in cost/expense reduction program which saved over $300,000 per year; replaced private brand label products with own formulations.

Created a polyurethane base plastic scouring pad.

Created a special detergent resistant wax for automobiles.

Engineering - Design

Designed and developed very low cost pumps to be mass produced on a jobbed out basis.

Successfully directed mechanism design group to permit marketing of product line which added $2 million to annual sales.

Developed 3 new machine designs and 3 new (patented) control systems.

Created a new manufacturing process to reduce product cost, which saved over $15,000 annually.

Developed, tooled and produced a more rugged model machine which improved Company's competitive market position.

Designed and established a first in the lighting field; an outdoor plastic ceiling fixture with an almost indestructible living hinge.

Reduced costs 20% on a current catalog item by introducing the glove molding principle as opposed to injection molding.

Engineering - Electrical

Completely revamped and simplified an automatic conveyor system layout, replacing an antiquated system. Acted as start-up engineer, to management's full satisfaction.

Under deadlines and trying conditions, designed and supervised installations of package power systems for offshore gathering platforms.

Prepared new operating procedures for equipment tune-up which decreased downtime substantially.

Saved 20% in original costs and service costs by numerically identifying wires and internal wiring diagrams.

Successfully handled electrical startup of plant.

Worked with vendor to prepare circuit and component layout for 20 punch presses.

Prepared initial electrical specifications for two foil rolling mills.

Utilized static switching to solve a chronic maintenance problem.

Engineering - Electronics

Replaced an electro-mechanical selecting system of 200 moving parts with one of no moving parts; saved $40,000 per year.

Trained electronic personnel and developed complete maintenance procedures and diagnostics programs for G.E. 4040 computer.

Helped increase average minimum daily repairs from 16 units/day/man to 19.

By careful inspection/rejection, reduced FM calibration errors by 5%.

Successfully completed wiring and assembly of public address console for ABC Building.

Designed and built a thorough system for evaluating speakers and speaker systems.

Designed and built a unique remote control center for 10 Arriflex cameras, to provide film footage for 360 degree screen projection at recent World's Fair.

Engineering - Industrial

Revised the parts recovery layout and operation; project cost $42,000 and brought annual savings of $180,000.

Initiated force reduction program; reduced staff by 38 people in 4 months without loss of production.

Improved material utilization and reduced scrap through inventory control methods.

Provided operational design for 3 new temperature controlled warehouses; now being built per recommendations.

Evaluated custodial methods and manpower; established cleaning standards and reduced annual operating costs approximately $48,000.

Assisted in the development of a computer linear programming model to determine line requirements and minimize corporate distribution costs.

Determined average pallet life and associated trip cost.

Determined the approximate corporate in-process inventory involving 7 plants.

Engineering - Maintenance

Reduced maintenance costs per unit from $10.00 to $8.23 by introducing work order system, preventive maintenance scheduling and scheduled repair down time.

Reduced mechanical maintenance cost from 1.34 to .83 manhours per 1,000 lbs. of metal produced; saved $18,000 annually.

Brought maintenance operations of Pittsburgh plant to new high level of standards.

Prepared new operating procedures for equipment tune-up, which decreased down time substantially.

Designed and built offices and service areas for mechanical and electrical departments.

Substantially reduced boiler down time for cleaning and repairs; power failures practically eliminated.

Over a16-year span, while coal costs quadrupled, plant cost per board ton only doubled.

Educated the firemen in proper techniques of firing with 3 fuels: coal, oil, gas.

Engineering - Mechanical

Saved $150,000 a year in labor by devising a unitized chassis for all 12" to 19" black and white portable TV's.

Have been granted 7 patents with 2 pending.

Helped develop ceramic slicing machines.

Produced all necessary hardware for EVR project.

Saved $200,000 a year for 3 years by a method of banding ORT tubes and an assembly system.

Developed new drive mechanisms, lighting systems and tuner mechanisms.

Designed and placed in production automatic equipment valued at $500,000.

Engineering - Project

Completed a thorough investigation of every aspect of Company entrance and participation in staple production for the building industry.

Insured proper installation and start-up services on all equipment by insisting on installation service purchase orders to all sub-suppliers.

Engineered and installed two $1 million projects; pressure casting of steel and vacuum degassing of steel.

Developed layout for South Works oxygen steel making facility.

Coordinated design efforts to complete $2 million pollution control equipment for an Electric Furnace Shop.

Engineering - Research and Development

Turned around a defunct 24-month augmentor development program; met program objectives in 6 months.

Closed a technology gap, with Company R & D now leading the field.

Expanded product line from 5 to 14; enlarged price range from $1,300-$3,500 to $595-$14,000.

Developed new products where acceptance resulted in 90% of sales dollars from products not in line 6 years ago.

Took command of the operation on an emergency basis, reorganized the Department, and molded it into an effective major unit of the Company.

Contributed in above areas of responsibility, with particular emphasis on testing and troubleshooting of prototype, to successful manufacture and test of solid state amplifier for positioning controls of synchro type.

Developed a product and method improvement with a demonstrated profit-increase potential of $100,000 per year.

Designed a package and a packaging method for meat patties which significantly prolonged shelf life.

Finance

Aided in the development of a statistical system to identify unexpected or unusual changes in the earnings performance of companies.

After financial analysis, made recommendation for purchase of $20 million company; recommendation accepted by management and purchase has proven successful.

Designed and administered the entire financial reporting system as the organization grew from 2 to 10 companies.

Built sales of a new product, Recreational Vehicle financing, from 0 to over $4 million.

Increased fee revenue of accounts under personal responsibility from $500,000 to $700,000 annually during the year of the price freeze.

Reduced annual recurring expenses $200,000 through work simplification, control procedures and staff reduction.

Increased customers' portfolio value 10% compared to a Dow Jones decline of over 10%.

Showed a gain for the Division in Direct Loan Outstandings of $700,000 and 365 customers for the year.

No loss in floor plan investments or capital loans during period as District Manager.

Successfully liquidated for $150,000 property with appraised value of $75,000.

Handled the negotiations for SBA loans totaling $350,000.

Financial Analysis

Recommended consolidation of 3 corporate accounting departments, after making cost studies.

Successfully installed effective variance reports.

Installed a computer time-sharing system for New Poduct/Business Analysis: provide 7-year P & L, RPI and breakeven points.

Improved procedures for better control of packaging costs.

Improved cash flow through better premium timetables and collection points.

Instigated an effective draft-payment system.

Handled post-completion audit of Gas Processing Plant modernization, a $1 million investment.

Handled post-completion audit for Company's acquisition of Bayview Oil Corporation, an $8 million acquisition.

General Management

Increased sales 400% in 2½ years.

Personally handled acquisition of a new plant in Indiana.

For more effective operations, reorganized the corporate structure and expanded top management of the Company.

As a marketing tool, introduced automated systems contracts and purchasing plans.

Built net worth from $25,000 to $300,000 in 5 years.

Increased sales volume from $10,000 to $300,000 annually.

Brought in an effective new management team—manufacturing manager and sales manager—and rebuilt sagging employee morale.

Established competitive bidding principle in Purchasing, saving $265,000 in 2 years.

In one year, $225,000 capital investment in equipment netted $196,000 savings in direct labor.

Designed and implemented new manufacturing standards and cost controls.

Saved $300,000 by rearranging and trimming product line.

Enhanced Company's competitive position by successfully negotiating two 3-year favorable union contracts.

Attained returns on investment up to 50% per annum. Consistently profitable.

Improved average return on assets from 32% to 48%.

Hospital/Nursing Center/Medical

Developed and installed operating economics in purchasing, reducing total supplies cost by over 5%.

Within 90 days of opening, haa capacity number of residents (120); maintained full occupancy.

Established good working liaison with all doctors.

Improved collection from 35%-50% to 85%-90%.

Set up effective training program for nurses aides.

Reduced linen losses drastically by developing a new linen service with effective controls.

Built and maintained excellent relationship between residents, families and employees.

Revised room rates to increase income, instituted insurance program, raised wage scale to meet local standards.

Established a fine reputation for the Center in the community; receive many referrals from hospitals, churches, welfare department, and private clubs.

Insurance

Became the first multi-million dollar producer in the history of the Company's district agencies.

Successfully handled complicated claim negotiations, to the satisfaction of major policy holders and the Company.

Named Agent of the Month for outstanding production; led a field force of 200 Agents nationwide.

Developed a successful small agency: from zero production and no agents to $4.5 million annual with 7 agents.

Achieved long-term fine relations with leading insurance companies.

Agency sold over $2.5 million in mutual fund sales.

In 2 years, increased licensed NASD agents from 62 to 304.

Provided solid basis for underwriting volume growth in these two lines never before experienced by the Agency.

Contributed substantially to increasing the insurance loss business by 30% in first 8 months.

Increased efficiency results of the Department by 41%, while claim volume increased 26%.

In the 3-year period, reduced customer complaints by 49%.

Inventory Control

Reduced total inventory investment by $50,000, while processing 20% more orders.

Reduced normal inventory by $100,000 by setting up blanket order programs with vendors.

Built inventory turnover to 12 times a year, through accurate and effective inventory controls.

Reduced inventory excesses yet maintained adequate stock to ship all orders upon receipt.

Established inventory control and vendor shipping schedule which maintained minimum inventory for maximum production.

Reduced inventory on hand by 30% with new perpetual inventory control plan.

Reduced the inventory write-off adjustment from $148,000 down to $8,000 by improved inventory controls and a better physical inventory system.

Was materially responsible for increasing annual inventory turnover from 3.5 to 6.0, resulting in a yearly savings of $100,000 in inventory investment.

Legal

Saved the Company $250,000 over a 3-year period in patent license renegotiation.

Realized a Company income of $25,000 from one patent used by others but previously unlicensed.

Made substantial contribution to the record of no major strikes in 3 years.

Led effective management seminars on labor relation and discipline problems.

Saved $150,000 for a client, on a tax refund case in Federal District Court.

Successfully organized approximately 50 corporations in various states.

Attracted substantial new business in areas of wills, trusts, and real estate transactions.

Recapitalized one bank holding company, made tender offer for part of shares, and arranged sale of balance of shares to buyer.

Acted as counsel to large insurance company in 2 private placements of notes with 2 NYSE companies.

Assisted in arranging financing for client selling goods in Japan.

Handled extensive corporate tax planning, with savings to clients.

Library

Maintained good staff morale, with resulting low personnel turnover.

Wrote two successful requests for Federal grants.

Prepared a new Personnel Manual, approved by the Board.

Prepared layout of stack and office areas in new building.

Handled budget planning and control.

Worked successfully with Library Board on policies.

Added substantial amount of books to update the collection.

Opened 3 new Branch Libraries in the County.

Stimulated County Board to provide Library with better quarters.

Marketing

Developed and introduced 3 new unique products representing 1,700,000 dozen annual sales and 5.8% profit before taxes.

Conducted major $150,000 consumer coupon effort; turned sales around from decline to 3% gain.

Introduced a replacement item under a new name; increased sales 39%.

Introduced bulk packaging system unique to industry, improving product quality and handling.

Set up effective analysis procedure to determine profitability of promotions.

Doubled market's sales volume, from $5 million to $10 million, in 2 years.

Established successful performance appraisal programs, one and five year marketing plans, and field training programs.

Increased region heavy duty truck market penetration from 10% to 40%, through new product development.

Established selective market oriented distribution plan, replacing geographic plan, and increased aftermarket volume by 19% in one year.

With opening of new store, produced an 87% increase in market penetration of lines for which personally responsible, as compared to store average of 56%.

In first year, achieved increases in *all* of these areas: sales, gross profit, turnover, return on inventory investment.

Personnel/Industrial Relations/Labor Relations

Developed and directed an overall personnel operation that successfully attracted and retained high caliber employees—without excessive salary structures or prohibitive total cost.

Instituted a successful salary administration program involving job descriptions, job classifications, job evaluation, rate ranges, and increase policies.

Reduced employee turnover from 5% to 2% a month.

Negotiated and renegotiated insurance coverages (life, hospitalization, major medical) to maintain the best benefit return per premium dollar, as well as company and employee acceptance and satisfaction.

Reduced time lag in filling non-exempt openings from 2-3 weeks to 1-5 days.

Upgraded caliber of employees through better interviewing techniques, screening, testing, and selection procedures.

Reduced turnover costs through effective selection, employee relations, communications, and department head training.

Substantial contribution to the record of no major strikes over the past 5 years.

Participated in many arbitration cases, with an 80-20 win-loss record.

Successfully negotiated two 3-year union contracts which allowed Company to remain competitive.

Successfully averted a potential wildcat strike.

Maintained good relationships with 3 of the largest local unions in the steel industry; no wildcat strikes.

Negotiated comprehensive local seniority agreement with 2000 member local production and maintenance union.

Plant Management

Saved $200,000 on a $5 million expense budget developed for increased schedule. Simultaneously improved quality 30%.

Developed follow-up performance reports for controlling plant operations: productivity; variable labor and expenses; packaging; raw materials and ingredients.

Implemented plant process control equipment resulting in $45,000 raw material savings in 6 months and estimated to obtain $150,000 additional savings in other areas each year.

Implemented raw material inventory control system resulting in reduction from 200 million to 150 million pounds.

Planned pre-production and labor leveling scheme which resulted in $90,000 labor and overtime savings and $70,000 storage savings annually.

Started up 2 new departments and expanded their production to 15 and 35 million pounds annually; around-the-clock operations.

Effected payroll savings of $40,000 per year by reducing direct labor from 14% to 13.5%.

Saved $15,000 a year in Shipping and Receiving through better labor utilization.

Police/Law Enforcement/Security

Division arrests kept at high level; court conviction rate high.

Awarded 6 Departmental Commendations and 30 Letters of Commendation.

Maintained the highest conviction rate in Traffic Division for cases involving driving under the influence of alcohol.

Initiated a training program for all officers, and for an additional 100-man reserve unit.

Trained the staff in modern methods of riot control, psychological and physical.

Unit under personal command is now recognized as the prototype for other departments across the country.

Accomplished a reduction in crime, upgraded the personnel assigned to the unit, and installed in subordinates the ability to make proper decisions.

Member of group which made largest seizure of marijuana in history of Midwest, 4,000 pounds Mexican.

Production Control

Was materially responsible for increasing annual inventory turnover from 3.5 to 6.0, resulting in a yearly savings of $100,000 in inventory investment.

Implemented a low cost control for low cost parts with a projected annual savings of $55,000.

Implemented a line leveling program which insured greater production continuity, increasing labor efficiency by over 11% plantwide.

Reduced reject-reworking time by over 15% by upgrading the caliber of employees through an effective efficiency rating system.

Built departmental operation to highest efficiency (157%) and lowest indirect labor ratio (19%) in Company's history.

Through personal patent, saved $20,000 annually by reducing component repair cost by 50%.

Reduced the inventory write-off adjustment by $140,000 ($148,000 down to $8,000) by improved inventory controls and a better physical inventory system.

Developed internal controls for lost-in-shop material, accomplishing a $13,000 ($17,000 to $4,000) savings in a 6-month period.

Established a master scheduling verification of contract status and production vs. shipment, changing in 9 months, a contract position from 30,000 units behind to 6,000 units ahead.

Public Relations

Secured immediate funds to meet current operating and payroll expenses and relieve the financial crisis with first 60 days effort.

Definitely improved corporate image at agencies under personal supervision.

Personally developed successful group sales campaigns.

Increased sales volume and profit margin over prior results.

Instituted monthly travel film presentations as public relations project to stimulate business.

Handled travel and tours from simple package arrangements to individually planned complex itineraries.

Arranged successful client company presentations before financial analyst groups.

Prepared fact books, data sheets, speeches and stockholder booklets.

Purchasing

Negotiated an 18% price reduction in packaging which saved $32,000 per year.

Reduced inventory investment $25,000 by establishing a stocking source and eliminated a 12-week lead time.

Set up a formal buying program for various items: policies, procedures, methods, files.

Established many new vendors, which broadened sources of supply, increased reliability and improved competitive price structure.

Anticipated shortages; secured adequate supplies of scarce items; placed items on annual booking.

Researched a new packaging program; reduced labor costs.

Instituted a direct-buy program which held food costs almost to levels of prior years.

Established new vendors which permitted more outside buying; machine time thus available for more profitable production items.

Profitably developed vendor changes.

Real Estate

Sold $600,000-$800,000 in residential sales during each of past 3 years.

Each year, sold 20 to 30 low and medium priced homes.

Developed a sound community relations image through quality operations plus personal effort in civic and realtor association activities.

Succeeded in materially reducing vacancy factors.

Substantially reduced operating expense ratios for managed properties from high to normal levels.

Achieved top status of return on investment of properties in the Region, compared to the other 5 U.S. Regions.

Rehabilitated properties and reduced collection problems.

Made solid improvement in management operations, including highly approved new budgeting and payroll procedures.

Built Company image with better client-agent relationships.

Opened 2 new 330 unit co-op apartments (new development); set up management and operating procedures.

Handled 500 weekly rental apartments in Ft. Lauderdale, Florida.

Completed detailed evaluations of 7 major metropolitan markets and located 6 specific communities for new installation developments.

Negotiated options, leases, contracts.

Awarded many remodeling and new construction contracts through negotiating ability combined with design knowledge.

Sales/Sales Management

Generated a sales increase of 50% the first 5 years by building greater wholesaler cooperation as well as adding new accounts.

Ranked 1, 2 or 3 in every sales program in every area worked during 3 years with the Company.

Always achieved 100% or more of Quota on every major item in the line.

Over a 2-year period, total dollar sales increased by 24% and dollars of marginal income increased by 59%.

Developed successful cold call techniques which accomplished 22% interviews and 10% closures—triple the norms for the industry.

In 3 years, built sales from 0 to $300,000 per year.

Maintained established business while increasing market penetration by 50%.

Successfully sold major chains including Jewel-Osco, A & P, National Tea, McKesson & Robbins, Walgreen Drugs.

Increased market penetration by 33% through restructuring territory and emphasizing sales programs; reduced territory costs by 15%.

Maintained a level of 100% of quota for 2 years, in spite of increased quotas and dealerization of territories.

Thoroughly reorganized the territory, with better product line balance, sales and profit.

Built and maintained a solid producing sales force of dedicated and enthusiastic people.

Social Work

Planned and implemented a summer camp program for all ages, including senior citizens.

Instituted a culture program for children in the Ida B. Wells Housing Project.

Established a tutoring program.

Recruited and trained youth and adult leadership volunteers.

Developed and presented a pilot project proposal for handling specific program problems; approval now pending.

Successfully enrolled many different ethnic groups in the program.

Successfully instituted on-the-job training as part of daily curriculum.

Handled criminal investigations on inmates of Boys School and Youth Center: made home evaluations; prepared social histories; interviewed inmates.

Handled public relations for the Department of Corrections; provided the primary link between the Department and the community.

Systems

Saved $20,000 annually with design and implementation of automated billing routine.

Prepared a purchase vs. lease analysis for the Sales Department which saved a account.

Effected large savings in space, time and money by use of microfilm for old records bringing order out of chaos.

Improved communications and work flow by design and installation of Purchasing Department floor plan (4 branches, 40 people).

Established a computer "Release of Orders" which reduced staff by 13 people, reduced processing time, speeded release of orders and permitted a balanced inventory.

Saved $8,000 annually by eliminating duplicate paper work on one simple operation.

Converted a 1401 tape operation to 360/30 65K, 5 disks, 2 tapes, 1 data cell.

Through systems and procedures study, reduced monthly computer time for Accounts Payable/Accounts Receivable from 25 hours to 15 hours.

Programmed an effective process control application for the laundry industry.

Supervised a group of programmers in implementing a statistical system in 30 days 15 days ahead of schedule.

Traffic/Warehousing

Negotiated truck freight rate adjustments that generated substantial savings each year

Expanded lumber handling from Arkansas and Louisiana by $300,000 a year.

Initiated program that built magnesium traffic by $250,000 and reduced the movement of empty equipment.

Designed and installed reporting and auditing procedure to control transportation expenses.

Designed (redesigned) warehouse (distribution center) facilities—saving $10,000 per year.

Reduced manpower requirements by 20% after Company warehousing concept changed.

Reduced labor force from 90 to 55 men through planning and better utilization of man power.

Developed new record system for Maintenance Department which saved $5,000 in clerical time in 5 years.

Increased volume 25% by diversifying business from one line to several lines.

Devised a system for unloading merchandise by pallets, which reduced costs and speeded deliveries.

Was expert witness for Association of Small Shippers against carriers; result was first the suspension and then cancellation of discriminatory Small Shipment Tariff.

section 6

resume samples

The following sample resumes are included to give you a concept of what a finished resume looks like. Do not copy a sample exactly. Compose your own resume for you as an individual.

INDEX

RUTH A. COOPER

3801 West Avenue
Chicago, Illinois 60636
Telephone: (312) 236-3800

OBJECTIVE	<u>Junior Accountant</u>

AREAS OF
KNOWLEDGE

Retail Sales   Mailroom Operations
Cash Handling   Office Procedures
Customer Relations   Stock Handling

PERSONAL

Birthdate: 4-1-59   Single
5'7"   160 lbs.   Excellent Health

EDUCATION

Austin High School, Chicago, Illinois
    Graduate 1977
Metropolitan School of Business, Chicago, Illinois - **2 years**
    AA Degree 1980 - B Average
    Over 40 Accounting hours

EDUCATIONAL
HIGHLIGHTS

<u>Metropolitan School of Business</u> - **2 years**

Graduate, Business Administration and Higher Accounting:
    Accounting   Federal Taxes
    Intermediate Accounting   Auditing
    Advanced Accounting   Municipal Accounting
    Cost Accounting   General Accounting

Additional Courses:
    Business Mathematics   Economics
    Business Law   Marketing
    Finance   Advertising
    Management   Data Processing

SUMMER AND
PART-TIME
EXPERIENCE
1979
1980
(Part time)

WIEBOLDT'S, INC., Chicago, Illinois.
Department store chain.

<u>Position:</u> Sales, Cashier

<u>Responsibilities:</u>
    -- Sell to the public, in various store areas.
    -- Handle cash sales and charge sales as Cashier in
       self-service hardware department.

Reason for Change: To secure permanent position in Accounting field after graduation.

Summer, 1976   KRAFT FOODS, Chicago, Illinois.

Position: Mailroom

Responsibilities:
-- Open, sort and deliver incoming mail.
-- Operate the Xerox machine.
-- Run errands, including bank deposits.
-- Collect and process outgoing mail.

Reason for Change: To attend school.

Feb., 1974
May, 1975
(Part-time
High School)

JEWEL FOOD STORES

Position: Stockroom

SALARY   Open to discussion.

TRAVEL   Readily agreeable to travel as required.

LOCATE   Willing to relocate for the right opportunity.

MILITARY   Not vulnerable to call.

AVAILABILITY   Immediate

INTERESTS   Tennis, bowling, spectator sports, reading.

REFERENCES   Mr. William Peters, Partner
                Brown and Peters, Certified Public Accountants
                5721 W. Peterson Avenue
                Chicago, Illinois 60643
                    Phone: (312) 678-9120

                Mrs. June Sampson, Supervisor
                Wieboldt's, Inc.
                1104 Church Street
                Chicago, Illinois 60635
                    Phone: (312) 216-7824

DONALD S. BURDETTE
342 West Bonn Street
St. Louis, Missouri 63100

OBJECTIVE   <u>Computer Operator/Programmer Trainee</u>

AREAS OF   Data Processing   Computer Operations
WORK   Payroll   Office Operations
EXPERIENCE   Billing   Inventory Control

PERSONAL   Birthdate: 1-18-55   Single
                     5'8"   170 lbs.   Excellent Health

SPECIAL   Computer/Programming School, St. Louis, Mo.
TRAINING   Certificate of Completion

EDUCATIONAL   <u>Data Processing</u>   <u>Management</u>
HIGHLIGHTS   Introduction to Data   Business Organization
                            Processing   and Administration
                         Computer-Programming   Principles of Management
                         Computer Hardware   Personnel Management and
                         Systems and Procedures   Industrial Relations
                         Tape, Disk   Principles of Production
                         Operating Systems   Management
                         Peripheral Hardware   Office Management
                         Computer Languages

WORK
EXPERIENCE
Jan., 1977   RED DEVIL MANUFACTURING CO., INC., St. Louis, Mo.
August, 1978   Manufacturer of screw machine products.   Sales $300,000.

                     <u>Position:</u> Office Clerk

1975   UNITED STATES ARMY
1976
                     <u>Position:</u> Private.   Honorable discharge.

Feb., 1974   CHICAGO MEDICAL INSTRUMENTS, Lincolnwood, Illinois.
August, 1975   Podiatry supply house.

                     <u>Position:</u> Invoice Clerk

July, 1973   W. H. SALISBURY & COMPANY, Chicago, Illinois.
Jan., 1974   Manufacturer of rubber products.

                     <u>Position:</u> Billing Clerk

AVAILABILITY   2 weeks' notice required.

RICHARD A. JAMES
1308 Washington Boulevard
Schiller Park, Illinois 60176
Telephone: (312) 678-8068

OBJECTIVE | <u>Management Position in Finance/Accounting, Leading to Higher Level Responsibility</u>

AREAS OF EXPERIENCE

Personal Selling
Human Relations
Public Contact
Cashiering

General Office Operations
Payroll Computation
Shipping
Receiving

PERSONAL

Birthdate: 7-15-54   Single
6'   180 lbs.   Excellent Health

EDUCATION

University of Michigan, Ann Arbor, Michigan
    B.S. Degree - Business Administration - Jan., 1979
    Major: Finance

Northwestern University, Evanston, Illinois
    Graduate School of Management
    MBA Degree to be awarded in June, 1981

EDUCATIONAL HIGHLIGHTS

NORTHWESTERN GRADUATE SCHOOL OF MANAGEMENT
Areas of Concentration: Accounting, Finance

<u>Accounting</u>
    Basic Accounting
    Cost Accounting
    Intermediate Accounting
    Advanced Accounting
    Contemporary Issues
    Planning for Mergers and
        Acquisitions
    Information Systems for
        Management Control
    Planning and Control
    Tax Law
    Business Law

<u>Finance</u>
    Basic Finance
    Money Markets
    Investments
    Portfolio Management
    Security Analysis

<u>Management</u>
    Individual and Group
        Behavior
    Operations Management
    Management and its
        Environment
    Management Policy

<u>Quantitative Methods</u>
    Linear Programming
    Management and the
        Computer
    Statistical Methods
    Quantitative Methods

<u>Economics</u>
    Micro-Economic Analysis
    Macro-Economic Analysis

<u>Marketing</u>
    Communication Methods

UNDERGRADUATE TRAINING

Management
Principles of Management
Office Management
Business Correspondence
Business Statistics

Finance
Corporation Finance
Business Law
Commercial Banking
Credit Management
Investments

Accounting
Principles of Accounting

Marketing
Principles of Marketing
Principles of Salesmanship
Principles of Advertising
Marketing Research
Marketing Management
   Problems
Traffic Management

Economics
Principles of Economics
Money and Banking

STUDENT
ACTIVITIES

Editor of "The Greek" - Fraternity and Sorority Monthly
   Newsletter
Interfraternity Council Representative
Marketing Club

WORK
EXPERIENCE
Summers

THE SMITH CORPORATION, Chicago, Illinois.

Position: Salesman, Cashier

THE HARVEY COMPANY, Chicago, Illinois.

Position: Payroll Clerk

ABC COMPANY, Ann Arbor, Michigan.

Position: Salesman, Shipping and Receiving

FORD MOTOR CO. (General Parts Div.), Saline, Mich.

Position: Quality Control Inspector

SALARY   Open to discussion in the $16,000-$18,000 range.

TRAVEL   Readily agreeable to travel as required.

LOCATE   Willing to relocate for the right opportunity.

AVAILABILITY   Immediate, after MBA degree awarded June, 1981

REFERENCES   References are available on request.

ARTHUR R. STONE

1520 Rock Road
Camden, New Jersey 08107
Telephone: (609) 751-0031

OBJECTIVE

<u>Attorney</u>

-- Law Firm, Mortgage Banking, Corporate Legal

AREAS OF
EXPERIENCE

Real Estate
Title Searches
Tax Buying
Real Estate Sales

Commodities Brokerage
Account Management

Criminal Law/Procedures
Trial Practice
Juvenile Law

Case Preparation
Trial Preparation
Court Appearances
Client Interviews
Legal Research
Brief Preparation and
  Drafting
Investigations
Office Management
Accounting Procedures

PERSONAL

Birthdate: 4-29-54
5'5"   145 lbs.

Single (Engaged)
Excellent Health

EDUCATION

Brandeis University, Waltham, Mass. - 4 years
    A.B. Degree: Cum Laude with Honors - 1977
        Major: Political Science
Rutgers State University School of Law, Camden, N. J.
    J.D. Degree to be awarded June, 1981

CERTIFICATION

Licensed Real Estate Broker: State of New Jersey

EDUCATIONAL
HIGHLIGHTS

RUTGERS STATE UNIVERSITY SCHOOL OF LAW
Juris Doctor Degree - June, 1981

Real Estate Law
Leases
Commercial Lending

Commodities and Securities
  Regulation

Trial Practice, Appeals
Juvenile Law
Criminal/Civil
  Procedures
Evidence

Contracts
Wills, Trusts

Corporate Law
Debtor-Creditor Law
Family Law, Taxes

Insurance Law
Administrative Law
  (Emphasis on F.C.C.)

UNDERGRADUATE STUDIES: Brandeis University

Pre-legal Courses
Economics (Micro, Macro)
Statistics
Linear Algebra
Computers
Sociology
History
Political Science

Honors Thesis
(1) American Military
    Assistance Program
    and Latin American
    Politics

STUDENT
ACTIVITIES

Rutgers State University School of Law

Minor Moot Court Competition: participant
Member, various student committees
Junior Bar Association
Freshman Moot Court
Federal Defender Program
American Bar Association: Law Student Division

Dean's List: One Semester
Papers on Tax Deeds and Tax Sales for possible publication

Brandeis University

Dean's List; Grade Point Average: 3.37 on a 4.0 Plan

National Debate Championship: First Place, Novice
    Division
Recipient, Hersz Debate Prize: two consecutive years
Director, Student Service Bureau
Tennis Team

EXPERIENCE
Jan., 1978
to Present
(Part time
concurrent)

BARRON CORPORATION, Camden, New Jersey.

Position: Real Estate Broker

Responsibilities:
    .. For this tax-buying firm: title searches and nego-
       tiations for buying and reselling vacant land.

Jan., 1978
to Present
(Part time
concurrent)

HERBERT MARKS, Attorney, Camden, New Jersey.

Position: Law Clerk

Responsibilities:
    .. Research, drafting briefs in Appellate Court,
       client interviews, court appearances, title searches,
       motion preparation, case preparation, investigations.

SALARY	Open to discussion, depending on position and potential.
TRAVEL	Any amount required by the position.
LOCATE	Plan to remain in the East.
AVAILABILITY	Immediately upon graduation June 15, 1981.
REFERENCES	References available upon request.
INTERESTS	Politics, art, reading, tennis.
COMMUNITY ACTIVITIES	Trenton Council on Foreign Relations Tennis Club Precinct worker in numerous political campaigns

JOHN W. THOMPSON

3112 Burke Avenue, Apt. 61
St. Paul, Minnesota 55105
Telephone: (612) 236-6597

<u>Family Address</u>

208 Aurora Avenue
Oak Park, Illinois 60304
Telephone: (312) 568-8588

OBJECTIVE	<u>Sales/Management Trainee</u>

-- Publisher, Manufacturer or Customer Service Organization

AREAS OF KNOWLEDGE

Over-the-Counter Sales

Office Procedures

Audio-Visual Techniques
    Overheads
    Tape Recorders
    Projectors

Office Equipment
    Duplicating
    Xerox
    Inserting Machines

PERSONAL

Birthdate: 7-5-57
6' 1"   200 lbs.

Single
Excellent Health

EDUCATION

College of St. Thomas, St. Paul, Minnesota - 4 years
    B.A. Degree
    Major: Political Science   Minor: Education
    Grade average: 3.2 on a 4.0 plan

EDUCATIONAL HIGHLIGHTS

UNDERGRADUATE TRAINING

Political Science
    National Government
    State and Local Government
    Comparative Government
    Public Administration
    International Relations
    Political Philosophy
    Introduction to Law
    Urban and Metropolitan
        Government

Economics
    Principles of Economics
       Micro and Macro

German

Mathematics

Fine Art
    Use and Techniques of
       Film Materials

Education
    Educational Philosophy
    Educational Techniques

Sociology

English

Science

STUDENT ACTIVITIES

Member of Tau Kappa Epsilon Social Fraternity (3 years)
    Pledge Trainer (1 year); Rush Chairman; Outstanding
    Pledge (Pledge President); Social Committee
Resident Student Council Representative

WORK
SUMMARY
(Part time during   BALDWIN-TAGEE GRAIN COMPANY, Minneapolis, Minn.
  college)   Grain exchange; elevators.

                       Position: Laborer

(Summers)   WALGREEN COMPANY, Berkeley, Illinois.
                       National drug store chain.

                       Position: Warehouseman

                       KROGER FOOD COMPANY, Northlake, Illinois.
                       Food chain stores.

                       Position: Warehouseman (Order Picker)

                       GAS LITE ILLINOIS, Subsidiary of Illinois Gas Company.
                       Supply and install gas lights and grills.

                       Position: Installation Helper

                       DANDELL SCAVENGER COMPANY, Glenview, Illinois.
                       Disposal service.

                       Position: Helper on Truck

SALARY   Open to discussion.

TRAVEL   Willing to travel on the job as required.

LOCATE   Agreeable to relocating.

AVAILABILITY   Immediate.

REFERENCES   References are available on request.

INTERESTS   Athletics, reading, politics, horticulture.

Dorothy M. Brown
8204 Robin Crest
Wheaton, Illinois 60187
Telephone: (312) 427-7104

OBJECTIVE

Accountant
        -- Manufacturing, Distribution or Service Firm

AREAS OF
KNOWLEDGE
AND
EXPERIENCE

General Accounting
Financial Statements
Consolidations
Management Reporting

Accounts Receivable
Accounts Payable
Invoicing
Freight Bills

Taxes: Payroll, Sales
        Corporate Income

Office Administration
Insurance
Personnel
Staff Supervision

Data Processing
Retail Stores

PERSONAL

Single
5' 8"   135 lbs.   Excellent Health
Willing to travel and relocate.

EDUCATION

DePaul University Evening School
        Accounting I and Accounting II
Institute for Individual Achievement, Inc.
        Computer Programming

EXPERIENCE
Jan., 1970
to Present

ABC COMPANY, Chicago, Illinois.
Leading department store.

Position: Accountant, Assistant to Controller

Earnings: $18,000 per year

Responsibilities:
    -- Prepare financial statements; supervise the monthly
    - closings; update analyses of selected ledger accounts;
       handle daily cash flow; supervise the Departmental
       staff of 6 employees.

1967
1970

SMITHFIELD FOODS CORPORATION, Morton Grove, Ill.

Position: Accountant, Retail Store Accounting Department

Responsibilities:
-- Personally handled accounting for certain retail grocery
   stores buying through Company Distribution Division;
   store employees numbered from 10 to 30; processed
   weekly reports for data processing; made closing
   entries and prepared financial statements; filed tax
   returns, quarterly payroll returns, monthly sales tax
   returns and corporate income tax returns.

1963
1967
EDUCATIONAL BOOKS, INC., Evanston, Illinois.
Textbook publishers. Annual sales volume $12 million.

Position: Office Manager, reporting to the Controller

Responsibilities:
-- Personal responsibility for office administration and
   all related office services; direct control of Accounting
   Department; supervision of 18 employees; prepare
   financial statements and reports; direct the preparation
   of state payroll tax returns; purchase office equipment,
   furniture, supplies; direct the personnel activities -
   recruitment, screening, testing, employment, training.

1957
1962
DINGHAM & WILLIAMS, Chicago, Illinois.
Public accounting firm.

Position: Bookkeeper and Accounting Supervisor

Responsibilities:
-- Full responsibility for all internal accounting functions
   of the office; prepare financial reports for Chicago
   offices; maintain cost and expense records of field and
   office auditors and consultants; control billing records,
   receipts and disbursement records, payroll and tax
   return data.

SALARY   Open to discussion, depending on position and potential.

AVAILABILITY   Immediate, after 2 weeks' notice.

TRAVEL   Agreeable to any amount required by the position.

LOCATE   Prefer to remain in the Chicago area; will relocate for
                the right potential.

PHYLLIS A. THOMAS

2030 Park Lane
Boston, Massachusetts 02115
Telephone: (617) 541-7933

OBJECTIVE	<u>Administrative Assistant</u>

**AREAS OF
KNOWLEDGE
AND
EXPERIENCE**

<u>Office Administration</u>
Office Operations
Procedures Planning
Staff Supervision, Training
Payroll Records
Correspondence, Memoranda
Manuals, Files, Records

<u>Meetings</u>
Planning, Execution
Hotel Liaison
Reservations
Meetings, Dinners, Protocol
Business and Social Functions
Staffing

<u>Travel, Communications</u>
Communications
Mail Distribution
Transportation Arrangements

<u>Personal Skills</u>
Staff Supervision
Effective Liaison
Work Scheduling
Letter Composition
Confidential Material
Figure Work
Executive's Bank
    Account

PERSONAL

Married, Two Adult Sons
5'4"   125 lbs.   Excellent Health

EDUCATION

Wellesley College, Wellesley, Massachusetts
    Liberal Arts - 2 years
Special Training:
    Patricia Stevens Modeling and Finishing School

**EXPERIENCE
1965
1980**

NATIONWIDE BROADCASTING CO., Boston, Mass.

<u>Position:</u>   Administrative Assistant and Personal
                Secretary to the President
                Assistant Corporate Secretary, Board of
                Directors

(1971-1980)

<u>Responsibilities:</u>

.. Served as Personal Secretary to the President,
and Secretarial Supervisor for all Nationwide
subsidiaries, including offices in Los Angeles,
Denver, New York and Tokyo.

.. As Administrative Assistant to the President, supervised the daily functioning of his three personal offices: Los Angeles, Denver, New York.

.. As Assistant Secretary on the Company Board of Directors, prepared monthly Board meeting reports; (elected an officer of Nationwide in 1973 -- the first woman to become an officer in a Boston broadcasting entity).

.. Received and responded to all the President's personal correspondence and phone calls; handled his personal banking and financial records; extensive preparation of confidential business and personal correspondence.

.. In the absence of the President, responsible for delegating the handling of all his mail to other executives, his secretaries or handling it personally.

.. Maintained payroll records and administered payroll changes for subordinates in all offices; supervised all original filing for other three offices.

.. Hosted and attended Company affairs and dinners; received dignitaries, business associates, government officials and personal friends of the President, and acted as host in his behalf.

Reason to Change: Resigned after completion of a leave of absence.

(1970-1971)   NATIONWIDE PRODUCTIONS COMPANY

(1965-1970)   NATIONWIDE TELEVISION SALES

1961   JON TURNER COMPANY, New York Advertising Agency.
1965
               Position: Estimator

SALARY   Commensurate responsibility-wise and salary-wise to that established in years of experience and dependability.

TRAVEL   Agreeable to any moderate amount of travel.

LOCATE   Prefer to remain in the Boston area.

AVAILABILITY   Immediate.

REFERENCES   References available upon request.

INTERESTS   American Women in Radio and Television.

VINCENT K. WOOD

1812 French Road
Toronto, Ontario, Canada
Telephone: (416) 234-3860

OBJECTIVE	<u>Purchasing and/or Office Services Management</u>

AREAS OF KNOWLEDGE

Purchasing Management
Departmental Administration
Hiring, Training,
   Supervision

Purchasing Systems and
   Procedures
Purchasing Policy Develop-
   ment
Purchasing Budgets

Vendor Finding, Evaluation,
   Selection
Negotiation, Contracts

Expediting

Purchase Quantity/
   Timing Control
Open End Ordering

Product Analysis
Materials Changes
Data Processing Appli-
   cation

Office Services: Mail,
   Printing, Duplica-
   ting, Files, Stock,
   PBX, Steno, Typing
Building Management
Office Layout, Con-
   struction

PERSONAL

Birthdate: 5-10-40   Married, One Child
5'11"   175 lbs.   Excellent Health

EDUCATION

University of Illinois - 2 years
   Mechanical Engineering
Wayne University Evening Division, Detroit, Michigan
   School of Business - 3 years

**EXPERIENCE
1971 to
Present**

WORLDWIDE EDUCATIONAL CORPORATION, Toronto,
Ontario. Manufacturers of educational films and related
materials.

<u>Responsibilities and Achievements:</u>

<u>Present Position:</u> Senior Buyer handling purchasing of:
printing; packaging, shipping and display materials;
phonograph records; recorded magnetic tapes; injection
molded plastics.
   -- Saved $6,000 initial investment and 6 weeks
      delivery time by having printer stock finished
      materials.

-- Reduced number of vendors from 100 to about 20.
-- Using current knowledge of cassettes, saved 15% on blanks, 25% on recorded units and 30% on containers in first year.

1979 Operating Manager
-- Had full responsibility for a successful general office move involving 200 people and 60,000 feet of space.
-- Saved $15,000 a year by redesigning new filmstrip package.
-- Saved $5,000 annually by changing supplier of stationery, and stocking by vendor.
-- Saved $3,000 a year with new vendor on phonograph record pressings.

1975 Office Manager
-- Effected substantial (up to $3,000) savings in telephone controls.
-- Modernized records retention and destruction program.
-- Saved about 1/3 of maintenance costs by eliminating 5 part-time employees and hiring an outside contractor.

1974 Assistant Operating Manager

1971 Administrative Assistant

Present Earnings: $18,000 plus bonus

Reason to Change: No opportunity for further advancement under present management practices.

Prior to 1971 NATIONAL MANUFACTURING COMPANY, Detroit, Mich.
Department Foreman (1959-1961)

DETROIT CASTINGS COMPANY, Detroit, Mich.
Department Foreman (1955-1959)

SALARY Receptive to salary discussion in $20,000 range.

TRAVEL Agreeable to amount normally consistent with the position.

LOCATE Prefer to remain in the Toronto area.

AVAILABILITY Immediate, after 2 weeks' notice.

EMPLOYER CONTACT Present employer may be contacted at any time.

LAWRENCE X. FRANKE

4100 Biscayne Blvd.
Miami, Florida 33132
Telephone: (305) 217-8304

OBJECTIVE   General Counsel

AREAS OF   Corporate Counsel, with broad experience in all phases
KNOWLEDGE   of corporate law and heavy trial work; taxes, real
                     estate, contracts and agreements of all types, anti-
                     trust, labor, management and product liability.

HIGHLIGHTS   * Successfully represented numerous corporate clients
OF   before Federal Agencies; represented a large single-
BACKGROUND   product manufacturer before Federal Agency result-
                       ing in a change in proposed law, thereby allowing
                       company to survive and prosper.

                     * Negotiated settlement of air pollution suit for large
                       foundry resulting in no fine and reasonable time to
                       install corrections.

                     * Obtained favorable verdicts in many labor cases
                       involving alleged NLRB violations.

                     * Successfully defended what may have been the largest
                       contract suit in history of door-to-door sales industry.

                     * Closed over 300 real estate transactions, commercial
                       and residential.

                     * Handled the organizing of over 100 corporations in
                       various states.

                     * Successfully handled extensive corporate tax planning.

                     * Satisfactorily resolved alleged anti-trust violations.

                     * Effectively handled numerous corporate product lia-
                       bility cases.

                     * Successfully prosecuted large claim of national bank
                       against bond carrier in employee theft case.

EXPERIENCE
1973 to
Present

BROWN, MILLER AND FRANKE, Miami, Florida.

<u>Position:</u> Partner

<u>Responsibilities:</u>
- .. Senior trial attorney, advisor to corporate clients, business sales and purchases.
- .. Federal and State taxes, business financing, labor matters.
- .. Anti-trust, real estate, securities regulations.
- .. Trade regulations, product liability, contracts.
- .. Estate administration, judicial proceedings of all types.

<u>Reason to Change:</u> To make full use of ability and experience as a successful practicing attorney; to bring to one corporation the complete range of legal and management service.

1966
1973

MILLER, GRAVES AND JONES, Miami, Florida.

<u>Position:</u> Associate and Partner

<u>Reason for Change:</u> To form a new partnership.

1961
1966

WILLIAMS, HELD, TOME AND FRANKE, Miami.

<u>Position:</u> Partner

<u>Reason for Change:</u> Joined a new law firm upon death of two of the partners; third partner semi-retired.

PERSONAL

Birthdate:	1-24-35	Married, Family
5'8"	170 lbs.	Excellent Health

EDUCATION

Marquette University, Milwaukee, Wisconsin - 4 years
    PhB. Degree
        Major: Philosophy   Minor: English
Marquette University, Milwaukee, Wisconsin
    J.D. (Doctor of Laws) Degree - 1961

CERTIFICATION

Licensed to practice before: U. S. Supreme Court, U. S. District Courts, all Courts of Florida and Wisconsin, various Federal and State Administrative Agencies.

PROFESSIONAL
MEMBERSHIPS

Florida, Wisconsin, Miami, Milwaukee and American Bar Associations; The Law Club; American Judicature Society; American Institute of Trial Lawyers.

ANDREW L. KENNEDY

6902 Elm Park Lane
Omaha, Nebraska 68501
Telephone: (402) 832-4216

OBJECTIVE

Assistant Service Manager or Auto Mechanic
-- Automobile/Truck Service Department

SUMMARY

A capable, customer-oriented auto mechanic -- with a
demonstrated ability and a desire to apply his technical
training and customer service knowledge and experience
to a new challenge.

MANAGEMENT
AND SALES
EXPERIENCE

Service Management

Service Expense
Work Scheduling
Tracing, Expediting

Service Personnel
  Recruitment
Training, Instructions

Employee Supervision

Customer Sales
Personal Selling to Key
  Accounts
Complaint Handling

Liaison:
  Vendor Representatives
  Manufacturers Represen-
  tives
  Customers

SPECIAL
TRAINING

Institute for Individual Achievement, Inc., Minneapolis, Mi
  Correspondence Training in Auto Mechanics
  Certificate Awarded

PERSONAL

Birthdate: 6-1-43
5' 8''   165 lbs.

Married, Family
Excellent Health

EMPLOYMENT
July, 1974
to Present

(Nov., 1978
to Present)

SUBURBAN DODGE-PLYMOUTH, INC., Omaha, Nebraska.
Sales/service of cars and trucks. Sales volume $600,000.

Position: Service Foreman, 2nd Shift

Earnings: $23,000 salary

Responsibilities:
  -- Full responsibility for 2nd shift operations; work sche
     duling, customer orders and relations.
  -- Direct the personnel; train apprentice mechanics;
     assist Parts Department man.

Achievements:
  -- Reduced lost time on repair work by 25%.
  -- Established a solid training program for apprentices.
  -- Reduced the customer complaints on service quality.

Reason to Change: Seek new opportunity to apply knowledge and experience; personal progress is limited with present shop.

(July, 1974
Nov., 1978)

Position: Head Mechanic

Responsibilities:
-- Assist the Service Manager who directed the complete Service Department facility; customer service, departmental management, service office administration, work flow and scheduling, expense control and reduction, warranty adjustments and billing, fleet maintenance program, customer billing.
-- Aid in supervising a staff of 5 people.
-- Handle all normal duties of a mechanic in auto repair work.

Achievements:
-- Built customer trust and confidence in the Service Department.
-- Helped increase shop gross income by about 25% in one year.

Nov., 1973
July, 1974

GARY CHEVROLET SALES AND SERVICE, Gary, Indiana. Chevrolet car and truck dealer.

Position: Journeyman Mechanic

Responsibilities and Achievements:
-- Mechanic handling auto repairs.
-- Assist the Service Manager as required.
-- Established an excellent repair service relationship with customers; trained 2 mechanics.

Reason for Change: Accepted new position as Head Mechanic.

July, 1968
Sept., 1973

GARY TRUCK COMPANY, Gary, Indiana. GMC truck sales and service.

Position: Assistant Service Manager

Responsibilities and Achievements:
-- Assist Service Manager in all operations of the Department.
-- Personally responsible for warranty repair work billing; set up facilities for proper storage of warranty parts.
-- Started as a mechanic and became Assistant Service Manager in 3-1/2 years.

| March, 1965 | CUTTLE MOTOR TRANSFER, East Chicago, Indiana. |
| March, 1968 | Trucking company operating in Metropolitan Chicago and interstate. Sales volume $2 million. |

<u>Position:</u> Road Service Troubleshooter

<u>Responsibilities:</u> Handle on-the-spot repairs to disabled vehicles in Chicago and surrounding areas.

SALARY	Open to discussion, depending on responsibilities of the job.
TRAVEL	Agreeable to the normal travel necessary to do the job right.
LOCATE	Will consider relocating for the right potential.
AVAILABILITY	1-2 weeks' notice required.
EMPLOYER CONTACT	Present employer is not aware of decision to consider change and may <u>not</u> be contacted at this time.
REFERENCES	References are available upon request.

HELEN MITCHELL

384 Greenway Road
Tucson, Arizona 85713
Telephone: (602) 771-4300

OBJECTIVE   Manager, Country Club or City Club

AREAS OF   Country Club   Kitchen Facilities
KNOWLEDGE   Clubhouse Operations   Bar and Lounge
                 Personal Hospitality
                                                 Outside Parties
                 Staff Supervision   Meeting Rooms
                 Hiring, Training   Buffets and Brunches
                 Work Planning, Scheduling   Golf Outings
                 Service Personnel   Locker Rooms
                 Personnel Allocation
                                                 Purchasing
                 Dining Room and Grills   Inventory Control
                 Menu Planning   Decorating

PERSONAL   Birthdate: 12-15-35   Divorced
                 5'9"   140 lbs. Excellent Health

EDUCATION   University of Colorado, Boulder, Colorado - 2 years

EXPERIENCE
March, 1970
to Present   DESERT COUNTRY CLUB, Tucson, Arizona.
                  Leading southwest country club. 400 members and
                  families.

                  Position: Catering Manager and Maitre-D

                  Earnings: $16,000 salary and commissions, plus annual
                  bonus, paid vacation, pension plan, paid life and hospitali-
                  zation insurance.

                  Responsibilities:
                      .. Manage all club dining areas (seating capacity -
                         400).
                      .. As club Hostess, to extend personal hospitality to
                         members and guests.
                      .. Handle catering for all affairs - food and beverage.
                      .. Hire, train and supervise all departmental personnel.
                      .. Personally handle purchasing.
                      .. Set up and execute all club and member affairs.
                      .. Arrange gourmet and specialized menus.

Achievements:
- .. Attained an overall level of efficiency and service that earned the satisfied approval of the membership and substantially increased membership participation.
- .. Upgraded the caliber of service through better personnel selection, training and supervision.
- .. Improved quality and presentation of food by personal attention and inspection; initiated new menu items.
- .. Regularly maintained costs within budget.

Reason to Change: To make full use of acquired knowledge and experience as a Club Manager.

Prior Experience

SANDS COUNTRY CLUB, Phoenix, Arizona.
260 members and families.

Position: Dining Room Manager, Catering Manager and (on a temporary basis) General Manager

Responsibilities:
- .. Complete charge of all dining areas and catering.
- .. Purchase food, beverages, equipment; maintain inventories.
- .. Handle staff supervision and employment.
- .. Make arrangements for special functions.

Achievements:
- .. Increased member participation by 20%.
- .. Was chosen by Board of Directors as temporary General Manager after resignation of previous manager; supervised clubhouse operations for 3 months.

Reason for Change: Better opportunity for personal growth.

FIRESIDE RESTAURANT, Denver, Colorado.

Position: Manager

Responsibilities:
- .. Set up and operate the restaurant, under general direction of the owner.
- .. Hire, train and supervise the full staff.
- .. Prepare daily menus and handle parties, coordinating all activities.
- .. Do all buying for the restaurant.

Achievements:
- .. Personal supervision of all food and preparation brought customer satisfaction and built sales.
- .. Established an overall feeling of hospitality.
- .. Kept costs at minimum by personal checking.

PINES RESTAURANT, Denver, Colorado.

Position: Dining Room Manager

Responsibilities:
.. Manage all dining areas, including full responsibility for all restaurant personnel; hiring and supervision.

Achievements:
.. Successful in increasing food sales and in establishing good customer relations.
.. Improved the staff caliber and morale by selective hiring.

SALARY	Open to discussion, depending on location, club size and potential.
TRAVEL	Agreeable to any amount of travel normally required.
LOCATE	Readily willing to relocate.
AVAILABILITY	30-60 days' notice required.
EMPLOYER CONTACT	Present employer is not aware of decision to change and may not be contacted at this time.
REFERENCES	Business and personal references are available upon request.
INTERESTS	Swimming, golf, gourmet cooking, reading, music, creative art.

KENNETH JASON
2305 Summit N. W.
Seattle, Washington 98125
Telephone: (206) 344-8165

AREAS OF
KNOWLEDGE

General Construction
   Institutional
   Residential
   Light Commercial

General Contracting
Sub-Contracting
Estimating

General Business Management
Public Relations

Financing
Mortgaging
Taxes, Permits

Personnel Supervision
Employment, Training

Sales Promotion
Advertising
Personal Sales
Customer Relations

PERSONAL

Birthdate: 8-18-35
6'   190 lbs.

Married, Family
Excellent Health

EDUCATION

Seattle Technical College, Seattle, Washington - 2 years
   Major: Building Construction
Special Training: Journeyman Carpenter Certificate

EXPERIENCE
1958 to
Present

KENNETH JASON, GENERAL CONTRACTOR, INC.,
Seattle, Washington.

Position: President, Owner and General Manager

Earnings: Average $25,000 per year

Responsibilities:
.. Full responsibility for operating the Company successfully and profitably, including delivering a
completed quality construction job which received
the customer's final approval.
.. Personal direct charge and the coordinating of all
aspects of the business operation:
      Building
      Estimating
      Sub-contracts
      Purchasing
      Construction Supervision
.. Maintenance of accurate business records, collections, clerical supervision and office operations.

      .. Handling legal and financial aspects of construction:
          Contracts
          Financing
          Permits
          Taxes
      .. Building sales volume through customer satisfaction, public and community relations, sales promotion and continuing good personal relationships with customers.

Achievements:

.. Successfully built a one-man business to substantial proportion through adherence to quality standards.

.. Constructed over 150 custom-built homes, ranging in value up to $150,000.

.. Completed a wide range of buildings including churches, industrial, commercial and others:

    Redeemer Lutheran Church, Everett, Washington
    Mercer Methodist Church, Mercer, Washington
    Christian Reformed Church, Tacoma, Washington
    First Reformed Church - Educational Wing,
        Seattle, Washington
    Calvary Baptist Church, Seattle, Washington
    Everett Christian Reformed Church, Everett, Wn.
    St. Paul's United Church of Christ - Educational
        Building, Olympia, Washington
    Bremerton Municipal Swimming Pool, Bremerton,
        Washington
    Olympia Swimming Pool-Bathhouse, Olympia, Wn.
    Boeing Company - Warehouse, Seattle, Washington

Reason to Change: Present economic conditions make it extremely difficult for a small contractor to do quality work at a profit.

SALARY	Open to discussion in general range of current earnings.
TRAVEL	Agreeable to the amount consistent with the position.
LOCATE	Prefer to remain in the Seattle area.
AVAILABILITY	Immediate.
REFERENCES	Business and personal references available upon request.

CHUNG PARK

3040 Laguna Avenue
San Francisco, California 94128
Telephone: (415) 233-6105

OBJECTIVE

<u>Controller</u>

HIGHLIGHTS
OF CAREER
BACKGROUND

* Financial Statements and Reporting
  .. Produced period-end financial reports 2 days
     faster; cut statement time by 20%.
  .. Designed, installed a new financial reporting
     system by plant (5 plants).

* Systems Efficiencies
  .. Developed an emergency parallel check proces-
     sing system; reduced check issuing time from
     5 days to 1 day for special cases.

* Cash Flow Improvement
  .. Designed a lock box system for cash collections;
     reduced deposit time an average of 3 days.

* Accounts Receivable
  .. Reduced accounts receivable by $70,000, with
     improved credit and collection policies.

* Inventory
  .. Reduced inventory by $125,000 through analysis
     of turnover, production and handling.

* Insurance
  .. Increased corporate blanket coverage $5 million.
     with additional premium cost of only $2,000.
  .. Saved continuing annual premiums of $5,000 per
     year; cancelled unnecessary policies, consoli-
     dated others.

AREAS OF
KNOWLEDGE

Controllership
Corporate Accounting
  Administration
Responsibility Accounting
Industrial Accounting
Branch Accounting
Cost Accounting

Financial Statements
Consolidations
Budgets, Forecasts, Planning

Auditing
Expense Control
Inventory/Material
  Control

Data Processing Usage
Insurance
Payroll, Taxes
Credit and Collections

Management Reporting
Supervision, Training

PERSONAL   Birthdate: 2-15-38   Married, Family
                  5'10"   Excellent Health
                  160 lbs.   Permanent U. S. Resident

EDUCATION   Stanford University, Stanford, California
                     M.S. Degree in Accounting - 1968
                  Korea University, Seoul, Korea
                     B.A. Degree - 1960
                        Major: Economics   Minor: Finance
                  Special Training Courses:
                     EDP Programming and Systems: IBM, Ernst and
                        Ernst, Universal American Corporation

EXPERIENCE
SUMMARY
March, 1971   UNIVERSAL AMERICAN CORPORATION, San Francisco.
to Present   Conglomerate. Sales volume $280 million.

(March, 1971   Position: Senior Internal Auditor
Nov., 1972
   and   Earnings: $29,000 salary plus $2,500 profit sharing
March, 1973
to Present)   Responsibilities:
                     .. Conduct operational and financial audits of subsidi-
                        aries and divisions of the Company, with emphasis
                        on manufacturing; areas include insurance, finan-
                        cial analysis, purchasing, credit and collection,
                        capital appropriation, inventory control.
                     .. Supervise and train Junior Auditors.

                  Reason to Change: Desire Controllership position; all
                  subsidiaries and Divisions of present company are out of
                  town.

Nov., 1972   MOIR AND DAVIS, LTD., Winnipeg, Canada.
March, 1973   Subsidiary of Universal American Corporation. Sulphur
                  processing. Sales $4.5 million.

                  Position: Acting Controller

                  Earnings: $20,000 plus $1,500 profit sharing

                  Responsibilities:
                     .. As Chief Financial Officer of the Company, handle
                        all Controllership and Treasury functions.
                     .. Manage cash flow, financial analysis, profit and
                        cost control.
                     .. Prepare management reports for Corporate.

                  Reason for Change: Transferred back to Universal
                  American.

May, 1970 March, 1971	THE GLOBE COMPANY, San Francisco. Vending machines. Sales $17 million.

Position: Chief Accountant

Responsibilities and Achievements:
- .. Supervise and manage corporate accounting functions; statements, cost accounting, payroll, accounts payable, inventory control, data processing reports and systems analysis.
- .. Implemented a process cost system, and inventory control system and an improved payroll system.

Reason for Change: Promised promotions did not materialize; company in financial difficulty.

1967 1970	ERNST & ERNST, San Francisco.

Position: In-Charge Accountant

Responsibilities: Handle balance sheet and income statement audits, SEC statement preparation, federal and state income taxes, and supervision and training of Junior Auditors. Analyze and improve EDP systems.

Reason for Change: To enter private industry toward a Controllership career.

1965 1967	NATIONAL BEARING COMPANY, San Francisco. Bearings manufacturer. Sales $5 million.

Position: Cost Accountant

Responsibilities: Prepare manufacturing budgets; make overhead and labor analyses; analyze job costs, EDP reports and systems.

Reason for Change: To join a CPA firm for public accounting experience.

SALARY	Open to discussion depending on position and potential.
TRAVEL	Within limits of reasonable requirements of the position.
LOCATE	Prefer to remain in the San Francisco area.
AVAILABILITY	30 days' notice required.
EMPLOYER CONTACT	Present employer is not aware of decision to consider change and may not be contacted at this time.
REFERENCES	References available upon request.

JUNE E. WALKER

7530 Walnut Hill
Dallas, Texas 75231
Telephone: (214) 632-2050

Personal

Birthdate: 5-6-44   Single
5'6"   115 lbs.   Excellent Health

University of Oklahoma, Norman, Oklahoma - B.A. Degree
SMU, Dallas, Texas: Supervisory Workshop for Women - 1974

Present Position

Credit Manager, after promotions from
        Collection and Adjustment Supervisor
        Collection Assistant
for the largest Division of a conglomerate.

Significant Achievements

Built good customer relations while reducing delinquent account
volume by 8%.

Kept all losses below the projected percentages of sales.

Established an effective procedure and set up a staff for expediting
customer deliveries to meet advertising break-dates.

Improved the handling of customer adjustments from a 3-4 week
delay to within 7-10 days.

Built an efficient and harmonious clerical staff by careful selection
and comprehensive training; reduced turnover and increased number
of promotable people.

Summary

A competent, supervisory manager -- with a demonstrated capability in credit/collection functions -- and a record of contributions
to operational profit.

Available after 2 weeks' notice.
Prefer to remain in the Dallas area.
Present employer may not be contacted at this time.

JOSEPH P. HICKS

36 Old Taylor Road
Scranton, Pennsylvania 18519
Telephone: (717) 754-1060

OBJECTIVE   MANAGER, DATA PROCESSING OPERATIONS

SUMMARY   A qualified, experienced Data Processing Manager, knowledgeable in the computer and systems fields -- who combines the necessary technical competence and administrative ability to get the job done.

EDUCATION   B.A., Economics, Pittsburgh University, with minors in Business Administration and Mathematics
IBM classes in Operations Management, Departmental Management, Programming
DPMA Seminars

EXPERIENCE
1971-Present

MANAGER, COMPUTER OPERATIONS, General Advertising, Inc., Scranton, Pennsylvania. Manage the Computer Operations of the Company on a 3-shift basis, 6-7 days per week. Responsible for production and quality control of computer reports, data preparation and systems coordination.

.. In 4 years, guided, managed and expanded the Department from IBM 360/30 to 370/145.
.. Reduced costly overtime substantially yet materially increased volume of processing.
.. Established a forms inventory control system which reduced forms cost and improved purchasing procedures and control.
.. Developed a competent staff with high morale and low turnover; in 4 years, lost only 6 computer operators from the Department.

1969-1971

MANAGER, DATA PROCESSING OPERATIONS, Will Youngman Corporation, Scranton. Overall management responsibilities for all operations of the Data Processing Department, work scheduling, production and control.

.. Designed almost all systems for the entire operation and programmed them.

.. Managed the Department successfully, with little
employee turnover while maintaining schedules.

.. Designed and programmed a coast-to-coast payroll
system, involving all federal, state and local taxes
then applicable.

1966-1969   SYSTEMS ANALYST, Pittsburgh Machine Company,
Pittsburgh, Pennsylvania. Plan, write and document
business oriented programs estimating marginal costs
involved in various operations of the Company.

1964-1966   IBM OPERATOR, Wells Fargo Company, Pittsburgh.
Wired unit record equipment and set up methods for
special operations.

PERSONAL   Birthdate: 4-21-43   6'1"   185 lbs.
Married, 2 Children   Excellent Health.
30 days' notice required. Will relocate.

Present employer is not aware of decision to consider
change and may not be contacted at this time.

85

WARREN C. CLINE

5311 Hillside Blvd.
Elizabeth, New Jersey 07252
Telephone: (201) 343-8170

Birthdate: 4-18-35   5'8"   160 lbs.
Married, 3 Children   Excellent Health

job
objective

To serve as MANAGER, NEW PRODUCTS PLANNING
AND DEVELOPMENT in any of the following areas:
plastics, rubbers, adhesives, related chemicals.

business
experience

ABC TIRE AND RUBBER CO., Elizabeth, New Jersey
    Manufacturer of tires, plastics, chemicals, rubber
    products, aerospace products.

Technical Director, Chemical Division (1973 to Present)
Responsibilities include overall management of Division
technical activities on current, new, or improved products and processes in areas of research, product and
process development, technical service, quality control.

.. Added $7 million annual sales to Division with 10
   new products.
.. Increased PVC plant output 20% and reduced unit
   cost with technological changes involving minimum
   investment.
.. Initiated and carried out personnel reductions of
   30% with no apparent loss of total effort.
.. Reduced total technical cost in a 3-year period
   while sales increased 18%.

Manager of Plastics Research
Responsibilities include management, through section
heads, of a staff of 70 involved in R&D programs on
materials, products and processes for water based coatings in paint, paper and textiles; polyesters, porous
plastics for coatings, and vinyl products.

.. Product and process improvements plus new product
   lines played major roles in enabling Chemical and
   Plastics Division to double sales in last 10 years.
.. Initiated and managed programs leading to new product line in textile latex area; current sales exceed
   70 million pounds annually.

Head, Condensation Polymers and Organic Chemicals Research

Responsibilities cover the planning in fields of urethane foams and elastomers, polyesters, polyethers and polysulfides, other polymers for forms, coatings and adhesives. Supervise staff of 14.

> .. Inventor and co-inventor of patents in urethane foam and other plastic areas; initiated programs in coated plastics and specialty elastomers; efforts producing over $60 million annual sales.

Senior Research Chemist

Responsibilities to pursue research and development activities in plastics.

> .. Inventor and co-inventor of numerous patents involving basic compositions, processes and products now contributing $45 million in annual sales at 4 plants.

other professional activities	American Marketing Association; American Chemical Society; ACS Chemical Marketing and Economics Division; ACS Rubber Division; Society of Plastics Engineers; Beta Gamma Sigma; Editorial Advisory Board, Journal of Cellular Plastics.
	Holder of over 15 U. S. and foreign patents; speaker and moderator at educational and professional meetings; author of numerous papers in journals and technical books, as well as marketing and management publications.
education	Massachusetts Institute of Technology, Cambridge, Mass. M.S. Degree - 1963 - Chemistry Columbia University, New York City B.S. Degree - 1961 - Chemistry, Mathematics
salary	Open to discussion in general range of present earnings.
travel	Agreeable to any amount required by position.
locate	Willing to relocate.
availability	30 days' notice required.
employer contact	Present employer is not aware of decision to consider change and may not be contacted at this time.

EUGENE S. ELLMAN

146 West Laurel Place
Shaker Heights, Ohio 44120
Telephone: (216) 383-9761

OBJECTIVE

<u>Director of Engineering, Chief Engineer or
Manager of Manufacturing/Production</u>
-- Leading to Senior Management Level

AREAS OF
KNOWLEDGE
AND
EXPERIENCE

Manufacturing Management: Production, Material,
Quality Control; Purchasing; Budgets; Personnel.

Engineering Management: R & D, Product Design,
Production and Tooling Methods; Cost Reduction;
Improvements.

Industries: Light Metal; Screw Machine and Press Products; Home Appliances; Pneumatic and Electric
Hand Tools; Components and Systems.

PERSONAL

Birthdate: 8-19-32   Married, Two Children
5' 10"   180 lbs.   Excellent Health

EDUCATION

Illinois Institute of Technology, Chicago, Ill. - 4 years
Degree: B.S. in Mechanical Engineering
Major: Mechanical Engineering
Minor: Research and Development

MEMBERSHIP

American Society of Mechanical Engineers

EXPERIENCE
1972 to
Present

CONTINENTAL ELECTRO-MAGNETICS, INC., Cleveland,
Ohio. Manufacturer of magnetic recording heads and
systems.

<u>Position:</u> Manager - Manufacturing and Mechanical
Engineering

<u>Earnings:</u> $28,000 salary

<u>Responsibilities:</u>
-- Direct the manufacture of mechanical components,
quality control, purchasing, production and material
control, scheduling.
-- Direct mechanical engineering, product design, production and tooling, methods, cost reduction, enginee
ing improvements.

Achievements:
  -- Developed new method of manufacturing a component part, resulting in cost reduction from 85 cents per piece to 15 cents per piece and amortization of tooling in less than a year.
  -- Designed, developed and fabricated custom tape recorder to record multiple tracks on 2" tape from 35 mm. masters.
  -- Designed for production from submitted prototypes a new recording machine, assuring further contracts for additional units.

Reason to Change: Seek more advanced responsibilities with a larger, better established company.

971
972

CAMEO PORTABLE TOOLS, INC., Durant, Ohio.
Makers of portable hand tools and fasteners. Annual sales $8 million.

Position: Engineering Manager

Responsibilities:
  -- Manage new product design, R & D, patents, manufacturing processing and cost control.
  -- Direct existing product improvement, testing, cost reduction.
  -- Purchase equipment and prepare budgets.

Achievements:
  -- Supervised a manufacturing cost reduction, design improvement program of existing products resulting in reductions of 15%-20%.
  -- Designed a portable, pneumatic tool to drive round head nails. Patent applied for. Potential sales - $400,000 annual.
  -- Designed a small pneumatic portable tool to drive fasteners as staples, brads and nails with interchangeable parts, jam clearance features, durability and simplicity. Cost of manufacture is 50% less than competitive models. Patents applied for. Potential sales - $1,000,000 annual.

Reason for Change: After merger, Management decision to eliminate duplication of engineering/manufacturing at two locations.

965
971

PORT-TOOL CORPORATION, Cleveland, Ohio.
Manufacturers of portable hand tools and fasteners. Sales volume $12 million.

<u>Position:</u> Chief Engineer, after promotion from Assistant Chief Engineer

<u>Achievements:</u>
-- Supervised an engineering group that completed the introduction of 7 new products within one year, through the stages of design, testing and pilot production, increasing annual sales by $3 million.
-- Developed more durable components, decreasing the cost of service and replacement by as much as 25%.

1956
1960

CHICAGO SCREW MANUFACTURING COMPANY, Chicago, Illinois. Manufacturers of standard and special screw machine products. Annual sales $15-20 million.

<u>Position:</u> Chief Engineer (Michigan Plant) after promotion from Associate Engineer (Chicago Plant)

<u>Achievements:</u>
-- Completed an analysis of a 40-year-old process to produce part blanks; designed tooling for multiple blanking from sheet in coil form, resulting in a capital expenditure of $300,000 and a reduction of production time from one month to 2 days for a run of one million pieces. Cost savings amortized expenditures in less than 3 years.
-- Engineering responsibility for a new venture in the manufacturing process of impact extrusion, which resulted in a profitable facility within the first year.

TRAVEL   Agreeable to any amount normally consistent with the position.

LOCATE   Prefer Cleveland area; willing to relocate for right potential.

AVAILABILITY   30 days' notice required.

EMPLOYER
CONTACT   Present employer is not aware of decision to change and may <u>not</u> be contacted at this time.

RAYMOND K. HELD

OBJECTIVE	<u>Electrical Engineer</u> Manufacturing Plant or Engineering Firm

AREAS OF KNOWLEDGE

Electrical Engineering	Variable Voltage Control
Project Engineering and	of D.C. Motors
Supervision	A.C. Motor Control
Maintenance Engineering	A.C. Control Relaying
and Supervision	Hydraulic Amplifiers
Design Drafting	Solid State Control
Construction	Numerical Control
Interviewing	Power Distribution
Purchasing	Lighting
Aluminum Manufacturing	X-Ray Gauges
Heavy Industry	Teaching Maintenance People

PERSONAL

175 lbs.	Single
5'8"	Excellent Health

EDUCATION

South Dakota School of Mines and Technology
    B.S.E.E. Degree
    B.S. Mining Degree
University of Iowa - Extension Courses

PROFESSIONAL MEMBERSHIP

Registered Professional Engineer, State of Colorado

**EXPERIENCE
1969 to
Present**

ALUMINUM PRODUCTS, INC., Denver, Colorado.

**(August, 1970
to Present)**

<u>Position:</u> Electrical Engineer - Dover, Delaware Plant

<u>Earnings:</u> $27,000 per year

<u>Responsibilities:</u>
- -- Work with electrical contractor to interpret drawings.
- -- Make installation drawings.
- -- Accept electrical equipment installations from the contractor and the equipment manufacturers.
- -- Hire and train maintenance electricians.

- Purchase equipment and supplies to maintain the plant electrical equipment during and after construction.
- Lay out and supervise the installation of work not completed by the electrical contractor.
- Set up preventative maintenance programs.

Achievements:
- Successfully handled electrical startup of plant.
- Maintained the electrical equipment with a minimum of downtime.
- Set up effective preventative maintenance programs.
- Had the privilege of watching the Dover Plant emerge from a peach orchard to a modern manufacturing plant.

(May, 1969
August, 1970)

Position: Electrical Engineer - Denver, Colorado Plant

Responsibilities:
- Handle plant type electrical engineering problems.
- Supervise maintenance electricians on a part-time basis.
- Work on electrical equipment specifications for the new plant at Dover, Delaware.

Achievements:
- Prepared initial electrical specifications for two foil rolling mills.
- Worked with vendor to prepare circuit and component layout for 20 punch presses.
- Worked with contractors' representatives to finalize electrical drawings for the Dover Plant buildings.
- Utilized static switching to solve a chronic maintenance problem.
- Worked with a manufacturer to develop the above-mentioned die-protection idea for punch presses at the Dover Plant.

Dec., 1968
April, 1969

COOR'S PORCELAIN COMPANY, Golden, Colorado.

Position: Electrical Engineer

Achievements: Solved some chronic maintenance problems and provided a fail-safe die protection circuit.

1962
1968

ALUMINUM COMPANY OF AMERICA

Position: Electrical Engineer - Alcoa Aluminum Sheet and Plate Mill, Davenport, Iowa.

Responsibilities:
  -- Handle electrical engineering work on heavy equip-
     ment in specific plant areas, such as Furnaces,
     Hot Line, Cold Mill and Plate Mill.
  -- Design circuits, handle material procurement,
     supervise installation, and check out projects.
  -- Do troubleshooting on mill equipment.

Achievements:
  -- Prepared tune-up and operating procedures for new
     equipment which decreased downtime considerably.
  -- Designed changes in circuitry which protected
     equipment and further decreased downtime.

TRAVEL   Agreeable to any amount normally consistent with an
                  Engineering position.

LOCATE   Willing to relocate.

AVAILABILITY   2 weeks' after date of hire.

REFERENCES   References available upon request.

ERNEST MC CALL

2130 Western Blvd.
Vancouver, British Columbia, Canada
Telephone: (604) 431-8174

OBJECTIVE

Industrial Engineering/Project Management

-- Problem Solving and Operational Analysis in
Areas of Production, Distribution, Marketing

AREAS OF
KNOWLEDGE

Industrial Engineering
Operations Analysis
Economic Analysis
Distribution Analysis

Production Control
Facilities Planning and
Construction
Facilities Expansion
Evaluation
Equipment Evaluation and
Cost Justification

Simulation Models
Computer Usage
Linear Programming
CPM, PERT
Replacement Theory

Work Measurement
Time Standards

In-Process Inventories
On-Line Accumulation

PERSONAL

Birthdate: 8-25-55   Single
6'2"   180 lbs.   Excellent Health

EDUCATION

University of Washington, Seattle, Washington
    M.S.I.E. Degree - 1978
    B.S.I.E. Degree - 1976
        Major: Industrial Engineering
        Minor: Business Management

EDUCATIONAL
HIGHLIGHTS

GRADUATE SCHOOL OF INDUSTRIAL ENGINEERING
Course Concentration: (1) Financial Analysis and
Control; (2) Business Management

Financial Control
Economic Decision Engineering
Financial Control
Engineering Economic Analysis

Related Courses
Quality Control
Operations Research
Economic Theory
Manufacturing Applications
    Data Processing

Business Management
Product Management
    Control
Small Company Case
    Analysis
Production Management
    Analysis

UNDERGRADUATE TRAINING

<u>Management</u>
Legal Background for Business
Business Law
Engineering Administration

<u>Systems Design</u>
Manufacturing Process
  Design
Systems Analysis & Design

<u>Production</u>
Automatic Control Systems
Production Control
Engineering Cost Analysis

<u>Psychology</u>
Psychology of Personality
Principles of Logic
Consumer Psychology

**PROFESSIONAL
MEMBERSHIP**   Institute of Industrial Engineering

**EXPERIENCE
July, 1978
to Present**

CANADIAN BEVERAGE, INC., Vancouver, B. C.
Food and beverage producer.

<u>Position:</u> Industrial Engineer

<u>Earnings:</u> $18,000 salary

<u>Responsibilities:</u>
- -- Consultant to wholesalers in design of new warehouses and improvement of existing facilities; specifically by improving layouts, material handling, equipment and operational procedures.
- -- Advisor to corporate owned branch warehouses; new and improved facilities as above, plus studies of manpower requirements and operational standards.
- -- Solve problems requiring industrial engineering techniques and evaluation in areas of production, distribution and marketing.

<u>Achievements:</u>
- -- Assisted over 20 wholesalers in the design of new warehouses or evaluation of existing facilities including operational flow, building characteristics, storage capacities, cost comparisons, material handling equipment specifications and corporate test results.
- -- Provided operational design for 3 new temperature controlled warehouses; now being built per recommendations.
- -- Evaluated custodial methods and manpower; established cleaning standards and reduced annual operating costs approximately $24,000.
- -- Personally identified the source of a problem causing congestion at the bulk can receiving dock; solution reduced overtime and trucking costs.

- -- Simulated the effects of on-line accumulation to reduce inventory and overtime.
- -- Assisted in the development of a computer linear programming model to determine line requirements and minimize corporate distribution costs.
- -- Assisted in the corporate effects evaluation of proposed increased pallet loads.
- -- Determined average pallet life and associated trip cost.
- -- Determined the approximate corporate in-process pallet inventory involving 4 plants.

Reason to Change: Seek a more responsible position with better opportunity for growth, broader experience and promotion potential.

Summer Work

KLINE'S SPORTING GOODS, Seattle, Washington. Manufacturer of sporting goods.

Position: Industrial Engineer

Responsibilities: Work evaluation and methods improvement of production operations.

Reason for Change: To return to school.

SALARY

Open to discussion; position itself of prime importance.

TRAVEL

Agreeable to any moderate amount of travel required.

LOCATE

Willing to relocate.

AVAILABILITY

3-4 weeks' notice required.

EMPLOYER CONTACT

Present employer is not aware of decision to consider change and may not be contacted at this time.

REFERENCES

References available upon request.

INTERESTS

Company Employee Association: Dept. representative; Volleyball captain; softball, bowling, basketball leagues.
Sports, flying, stamp collecting.

TIMOTHY O'SHEA

7512 Memorial Drive
Wilmington, Delaware 19898
Telephone: (302) 503-6052

OBJECTIVE	Mechanical Engineer
AREAS OF KNOWLEDGE	Engineering Management: R&D, Product Design Production and Tooling Methods; Cost Reduction.
	Manufacturing Management: Production, Material, Quality Control; Purchasing; Budgets; Personnel.
	Industries: Light Metal; Screw Machine and Press Products; Home Appliances, Pneumatic and Electric Hand Tools; Fasteners for the building industry.
PERSONAL	Birthdate: 6-7-35 Single 5'8" 145 lbs. Excellent Health
EDUCATION	Massachusetts Institute of Technology, Cambridge Degree: B.S. in Mechanical Engineering
PROFESSIONAL MEMBERSHIP	American Society of Mechanical Engineers
EXPERIENCE March, 1974 to Present	ATLANTIC DIVISION of LCW CORPORATION, Wilmington, Delaware. Manufacturers of fasteners for the building industry.

Position: Senior Project Engineer

Responsibilities:
-- Develop new products; new hand tools and fasteners for the building industry.
-- Investigate new processes for the improvement of existing products.

Achievements:
-- Developed new concepts for fasteners and hand tools warranting patent application.
-- Completed a thorough investigation of every aspect of Company entrance and participation in staple production for the building industry.

Reason for Change: Staff reduction due to economic conditions.

1970
1974

INTERNATIONAL MAGNETICS, INC., Wilmington, Del.
Manufacturer of recording instruments and components.

Position: Manager - Manufacturing and Mechanical
Engineering

Responsibilities:
-- Direct the manufacture of mechanical components,
quality control, purchasing, production, material
control, scheduling.
-- Direct mechanical engineering, product design,
production and tooling, methods, cost reduction,
engineering improvements.
-- Hire and train personnel, manage budgets, make
cost analyses and handle bid proposals.

Achievements:
-- Developed new method of manufacturing pole pieces,
resulting in cost reduction and amortization of tooling in less than a year.
-- Designed, developed and fabricated custom tape
recorder to record 24 tracks on 2" tape from 35 mm.
masters.
-- Designed for production from submitted prototypes
a braille machine, assuring further contracts for
additional units.

Reason for Change: Sought more advanced responsibilities
with a larger, better established company, offering growth
potential.

1968
1970

ACE, INC., Broadview, Connecticut.
Makers of portable hand tools and fasteners.

Position: Engineering Manager

Responsibilities:
-- Manage new product design, R & D, patents, manu-
facturing processing and cost control.
-- Direct existing product improvement, testing, cost
reduction.
-- Purchase equipment and prepare budgets.

Achievements:
-- Supervised a manufacturing cost reduction, design
improvement program of existing products; savings
of 15%-20%.
-- Designed a portable, pneumatic tool to drive round
head nails. Lighter, smaller, simpler and less expensive than competitive models. Patent applied for.

- Devised a means of cohering nails in coil form, permitting greater load capacity in a smaller space than competitive methods. Equipment for cohering was one-tenth the cost of competitive equipment. Potential sales $1 million.
- Devised a method of cohering staple material in a compact space to be formed and used as a staple in a unique manner.

Reason for Change: After merger, Management decision to eliminate duplication of engineering/manufacturing at two locations.

1962 1968	FASTENER CORPORATION, Wilmington, Delaware. Manufacturers of portable hand tools and fasteners.

Position: Chief Engineer

Responsibilities: Basically similar to 1968-1970 duties.

Achievements:
- Supervised an engineering group that completed the introduction of 7 new products within one year; design, testing and pilot production, increasing annual sales by $5 million.
- Developed more durable components, decreasing the cost of service and replacement by as much as 25%.

1959 1962	JOHNSON MANUFACTURING COMPANY, Chicago, Illinois. Manufacturers of standard and special screw machine products.

Position: Chief Engineer (Waukegan, Ill. Plant)

Responsibilities: Modernize plant manufacturing facilities; develop processes and tooling; do cost analysis and reduction. Purchase equipment and tooling. Manage the Engineering Department -- process and design. Establish a plant, select and train personnel.

Achievements:
- Engineering responsibility for a new venture in the manufacturing process of impact extrusion, which resulted in a profitable facility within the first year.

SALARY	Receptive to salary discussion in the general range of current earnings.
TRAVEL	Agreeable to any amount normally consistent with position.
LOCATE	Prefer Wilmington area; willing to relocate for right potential.

RUSSELL G. RAY
1040 Stone Road
Rochester, New York 14621
Telephone: (716) 423-8561

OBJECTIVE Sales/Marketing -- Food or Related Industry

HIGHLIGHTS OF CAREER

As Vice President and Director of Company Operations
* Built food chain units from 4 to 20 with negotiations under way for additional units nationwide.
* Revised and improved training programs for both company and franchisee personnel; worked with Stanford University Training Division.
* Established a base of trained manpower for expansion; set up company operations as cores for regional advertising/promotion programs.

As Area Director
* Originated the "Chicken Pickin Wednesday" special dinner now nationwide in the chain.
* Increased Area sales from $3 million to $4.5 million in 18 months.
* Hired and trained 6 Area Managers, one Area Director, one Catering Director, one Assistant Training Instructor.
* Introduced and promoted Extra Crispy Chicken to Philadelphia market; built sales from 0 to 36% of total sales volume.

As Coordinator of Field Service
* Directed the planning and pilot operation of a Roast Beef program; store modification, staff training.
* Established a successful bonus system for company management staff.
* Handled liaison with Company's producer of annual convention (2,000 attendance); personally managed local regional mini-conventions.

AREAS OF KNOWLEDGE AND EXPERIENCE

Chain Management	Staff Supervision
Fast Food Operations	Personal Selling of Key Accounts
Sales Management	Customer Relations
Departmental Administration	Purchasing
Systems Administration	
Sales/Business Promotion	Inventory Control
Forecasting	Restaurant Management
Training	Trade Shows

PERSONAL	Birthdate: 9-15-31	Divorced, Two Children
	6' 200 lbs.	Excellent Health

EDUCATION University of Rochester, Rochester, New York
       MBA Degree - 1966
      Cornell University, Ithaca, New York
       BS Degree - 1955

PROFESSIONAL Sales Marketing Executives
MEMBERSHIPS Cornell Society of Hotelmen

EXPERIENCE
SUMMARY
1968 to   MARIO'S, INC., Rochester, New York.
Present   Pizza chain. 300 plus units. Sales volume $10 million.

      Position: Vice President and Director of Company
            Operations

      Responsibilities:
        -- Full responsibility for company growth and profit.
        -- Direct an executive staff of 13 management people
          controlling operations of the Company.
        -- Supervise all business functions; operations, sales,
          promotion, purchasing, financial.
        -- Evaluate new products and equipment; design modi-
          fications.

1962
1968   SOUTHERN FRIED CHICKEN, INC., Rochester, N. Y.

      Position: Area Director - Rochester and Philadelphia

      Responsibilities:
        -- Direct the Area operations: 22 chicken stores,
          with 310 employees, grossing $6 million, plus a
          pancake house restaurant doing $700,000.
        -- Supervise and train 46 Managers and Assistant
          Managers, plus Catering and Training Directors
          and other support personnel.
        -- Full responsibility for sales, profit, financial
          planning, cost control, inventory control and work
          plans.

1958
1962   CHAMPION CORPORATION, Albany, New York.
      Major fast food limited menu chain. 3,000 units.

      Position: Coordinator of Field Service

Responsibilities:
-- Plan and implement corporate decisions on
national level.
-- Coordinate communications from Regional operations managers to insure adherence to policies,
standards and procedures.
-- Analyze and establish Regional budgets; capital,
expense.

1955 1958	DEL-RAY'S RESTAURANT, Albany, New York. Limited menu fast food restaurant. Annual volume $125,000.

Position: Partner

Responsibilities:
-- Handle all management and operations supervision;
partner handled some administrative duties while
acting as General Counsel of the parent corporation.
-- Reversed a downward sales trend and stabilized a
deteriorating situation.

SALARY	Open to discussion, depending on position and potential.
TRAVEL	Agreeable to unlimited travel.
LOCATE	Willing to relocate.
AVAILABILITY	4-6 weeks notice required.

WILLIAM E. ROBERTS

333 E. 92nd Street
New York City, New York 10028
Telephone: (212) 681-2234

OBJECTIVE   <u>Director: Profit Planning or Financial Planning</u>

AREAS OF   Profit Planning   Time Sharing Applications
KNOWLEDGE   Financial Analysis   Responsibility Accounting
AND   Budgets   Consolidation Accounting
EXPERIENCE
                   Long Range Planning   Cost Centers
                   Forecasting
                                                  Stock Analysis
                   Cash Flow   Chart Analysis
                   Capital Investment

PERSONAL   Birthdate: 10-13-35   Married, One Child
                   5'10"   175 lbs.   Excellent Health

EDUCATION   Columbia University, New York City - 4 years
                       B.S. Degree
                           Major: Business Administration   Minor: Finance

                   Special Training: New York Institute of Finance

PROFESSIONAL   Planning Executives Institute: Council Member
MEMBERSHIPS   Corporate Planning Council

FINANCIAL
PLANNING
EXPERIENCE

1971 to   GOLDEN INTERNATIONAL, Division of A.M.C. Indus-
Present   tries, New York City. Manufacturers of automotive parts
                   and recreational vehicles. Sales volume over $100 million.

                   <u>Position:</u> Corporate Budget Manager

                   <u>Responsibilities:</u>
                       -- Coordinate and consolidate all data for annual
                          profit plan and 5-year profit plan; assist in estab-
                          lishing objectives and goals.
                       -- Prepare capital investment analysis; make project
                          evaluation to insure validity; recommend buy or not
                          buy decisions.
                       -- Handle special projects for Controller and Vice
                          President, Administration.

Achievements:
- Installed an effective responsibility accounting system providing pertinent data for management decisions.
- Developed and installed the budget and general ledger system using computer time sharing.
- Revised and improved the chart of accounts.
- Made statistical and time sharing models.

Reason to Change: Change in management resulting in staff reduction.

1966
1971

RUBENSTEIN INDUSTRIES, New York City.
Toiletries manufacturer. Sales volume $8.5 million.

Position: Senior Budget Analyst

Responsibilities:
- Install annual profit forecast plan; develop graphs and charts for financial program presentation.
- Consolidate monthly forecasts.
- Produce monthly variance reports.
- Maintain general ledger account number compatibility for all company Divisions.

Achievements:
- Established responsibility accounting for corporate cost centers; identified and highlighted profitable areas and problem areas.
- Reduced monthly closing time schedule by 3 days by installing general ledger system on data processing.
- Served as President, Secretary and Treasurer of Credit Union.

Reason for Change: Accepted a position which offered more opportunity for advancement and greater earnings.

1964
1966

UNIVERSAL GRAIN COMPANY, New York City.
Grain and flour milling company and commodity brokerage firm.

Position: Market Analyst and Account Supervisor

Responsibilities and Achievements:
- Act as firm's commodity analyst; prepare commodity charts and market letters.
- Supervise the margin accounts.
- Successfully supervised the installation of margin accounts on data processing; maintained all records and reports submitted to the Commodity and Exchange Authority.

BROKERAGE EXPERIENCE

1963-1964

THOMPSON-STONE, New York City. Stock brokers.

Position: Registered Representative and Security Trader

Responsibilities:
-- Execute security and commodity orders; maintain records of commodity trades.

1962-1963

MILLS AND CROWTHER, New York City. Stock brokers.

Position: Registered Representative and Security Trader

Responsibilities:
-- Maintain markets for the Over-the-Counter stocks; execute orders in the market and on various stock exchanges.

1960-1962

KING, BANKS AND JONES, New York City. Stock brokers.

Position: Registered Representative

Responsibilities:
-- Execute orders on stock exchanges and through the Over-the-Counter market; supervision of all listed transactions.

1959-1960

C. F. CHILDS, New York City. Government bond and security dealer.

Position: Securities Order Clerk and Account Executive

Responsibilities:
-- Maintain branch office records and balance sheet.
-- Assisted in handling business solicitation with banks in New Jersey and Pennsylvania.

SALARY — Open to discussion, depending on position and potential.

TRAVEL — Agreeable to moderate travel, up to 10%-20%.

LOCATE — Prefer to remain in New York City area.

AVAILABILITY — 3-4 weeks' notice required.

EMPLOYER CONTACT — Present employer is aware of change and may be contacted at any time.

REFERENCES — References available upon request.

RALPH M. COLE

235 Peachtree Road
Atlanta, Georgia 30308
Telephone: (404) 723-8171

Objective

Challenging Responsibility in Creative Senior Management
General Management
Sales/Marketing Management

Career Achievements

GENERAL MANAGEMENT
.. As a Regional V.P., was Senior Company Officer
in a 14-state area; $300 million in annual production
with sales staff of 800.
.. Directed successful opening of 8 new agencies.
.. Built Honolulu agency from zero to $14 million
volume in 3 years; fastest growth of any new agency
in the Company.

SALES/MARKETING
.. Achieved 40% sales growth the first year managing
current agency; 1975 growth to date 43% over 1974;
on schedule for $200,000 plus in first year commis-
sions in 1975, excluding group insurance.
.. As Field Sales Director, led the entire Company for
2 years in percent of quota.
.. Honolulu agency premium income increased from
zero to $285,000 in 3 years.

MANPOWER RECRUITMENT/DEVELOPMENT
.. As Regional Vice President, developed 3 Managers
now Company V.P.s, along with 2 Managers currently
Assistant V.P.s, achieved recruitment quotas 3 consecutive years.
.. As Regional V.P., recruited over 40 men for a
management training program.
.. As Manager of Company's first Hawaiian agency, had
8 men make the Million Dollar Round Table; had a 76%
manpower retention rate over 3 years.
.. As Agency Manager, recruited 43 men in last 3 years,
with triple the industry retention rate.

Work History

1960-Present   JOHN HANCOCK INSURANCE COMPANY

<u>Agency Manager</u> - Atlanta (1970 to Present)
(8th in size among 200 Company agencies)

<u>Regional Vice President</u> - San Francisco (1966-1970)
(14 western states - 27 full managing agencies)

<u>Field Sales Director:</u> Eastern Region (New York)
South Pacific Region (Los Angeles) (1964-1966)

<u>Agency Manager</u> - Honolulu (1961-1964)

<u>Sales Representative and Assistant Manager</u> -
San Diego (1960-1961)

Professional Memberships

National Association of Life Underwriters
General Agents and Managers Association
National Association of Security Dealers

Personal

Married
6'   180 lbs.   Excellent Health
Will travel.   Will relocate.

MICHAEL P. WILSON

7520 St. Charles
New Orleans, Louisiana 70130
Telephone: (504) 662-0451

OBJECTIVE

Executive career in portfolio management with the opportunity to pursue investment research.

PERSONAL DATA

Single   Height: 5'11"   Weight: 175 lbs.
Birthdate: August 24, 1943

EXPERIENCE

INVESTMENT OFFICER of Southwestern Trust & Savings Bank, serving the Employees Trust Department. Joined the bank in August, 1970, as a portfolio manager-research analyst. Current responsibilities include management of pension and profit sharing trusts which entails the establishment of investment objectives and the selection of issues to produce results satisfactorily to the customer.

.... Accomplishments include the successful management of
    trust accounts approximating $350 million including the
    bank's largest fund (its fee is calculated on the basis of
    an incentive formula) and initiation of research which led
    to the trust use of two securities, Standard Paint and
    AMK Corporation.

ASSISTANT PORTFOLIO MANAGER, for pension funds, August, 1968 to July, 1970, with the Chase Manhattan Bank. Initial responsibility included exposure to investment research as a junior auto-rubber analyst. Became co-manager for the Ford Retirement Trust and was designated as manager of the Chase's special capital fund.

Part Time: 1965-1968, founder and manager of College Record Sales, New York City. Revenues of component and phonograph record sales reached $15,000 annually.

EDUCATION

Columbia University -- Graduate School of Business -- Degree of Master of Business Administration May, 1970, with concentrations in finance and marketing. Member of Alpha Kappa Psi, professional business fraternity.

Carleton College, A. B. degree in June, 1966 with major in economics and strong minor in psychology. Photographic editor of Carleton's 1965 Yearbook. Expenses financed by summer employment and personal portfolio management.

AFFILIATIONS

Serving on Arrangements Committee of New Orleans Security Analysts Society.

New Orleans Area Representative for Carleton College.

PERSONAL BACKGROUND

Native of New York City. Avocations: Music, numismatics, photography. Enjoy traveling: recent journeys include Middle East 1972, East Africa 1971 and Orient and Far East 1968.

SALARY REQUIREMENT:

Open to discussion in the range of $28,000 to $30,000 based upon the challenge of the position and in relation to future potential.

References will be furnished upon request.

COL. PAUL R. YOUNGER, U.S.M.C.

1002 Lunar Drive
Glenview, Illinois 60025
Telephone: (312) 724-4059

OBJECTIVE   Airport Management: Senior Administrator

SUMMARY   A fully qualified U. S. Marine Corps officer with a
                   solid background of performance and administrative
                   competence; leaving military service to move into
                   comparable civilian administration.

AREAS OF   General Business   Airfield Control Pro-
KNOWLEDGE   Administration   cedures Tower,
                   Procedures Determination   F.A.A.
                   Budgeting   Transport and Light
                                                   Aircraft: Operation
                   Personnel Training/Supervision Procedures
                   Systems Supervision   Airport Equipment
                   Employee Relations   Emergency, Fire-
                                                    fighting
                   Meteorology

PERSONAL   Birthdate: 8-25-27   Married, Family
                   5'8"   160 lbs.   Excellent Health

EDUCATION   University of Nebraska, Lincoln, Nebraska
                      B.A. Degree in Liberal Arts - 1955
                        Major: Finance

                   U. S. Marine Corps Command and Staff College
                      Degrees not awarded. Training equivalent to M.A.

                   Special Training: Senior Officers Computer Seminar

PILOT
QUALIFICATIONS
                   Qualified in 20 different aircraft (in 20 years).
                   Flown over 6,000 hours (4,000 in transport aircraft).
                   Prop, jet, single and multi-engine aircraft.
                   Domestic and international routes.
                   Highest instrument rating for last 15 years.
                   FAA Certification: multi-engine and instrument

EXPERIENCE
1953 to
Present

UNITED STATES MARINE CORPS. Career Officer with bulk of experience in leadership, administration and aircraft operations.

(1971 to
Present)

Location: HQ Staff, 4th Marine Air Wing/Marine Air
                Reserve Training Command, Glenview, Illinois

Position: Assistant Chief of Staff, Personnel Matters
                (Col.)
                Assistant to Director of Operations and
                Training (Col.)

Responsibilities:
.. Direct and supervise 24 recruiting offices with 48
   personnel to recruit 1500 Marine Corps Reservists
   per year.
.. Establish policy and implement program for placement of 2600 regular duty Marines for 24 U. S. sub-
   commands.
.. Advise Commanding General on all personnel
   matters; represent him as guest speaker at various
   functions.
.. Supervise training of 900 pilots, using 350 aircraft.

Achievements:
.. Reversed trend of resignations exceeding enlistments.
.. Restructured the organization on national scope;
   reduced staff by 315.
.. Successfully directed 3-day seminar of 100 field
   commanders.

Reason for Change: Desire a new challenge in civilian
activity after completion of military career.

(1969-1971)

Location: Marine Air Group, Hawaii

Position: Executive Officer, 2nd in command (Lt. Col.)

Responsibilities:
.. Direct the HQ staff of 40 officers and 90 enlisted
   men; assume responsibilities of Group Commanding
   Officer in his absence; advise the C. O. on all
   matters; implement policies.
.. Supervise budget; supervise pilot training (160 pilots).

Achievements:
.. Group equalled or exceeded all training requirements;
   one Squadron recognized as best in Marine Corps in
   1971.
.. Group recognized for achieving highest state of com-
   bat readiness of all Groups in Western U. S.

| (1968-1969) | Location: Marine Airbase Squadron, Hawaii |
| | Position: Commanding Officer (Lt. Colonel) |

Responsibilities:
- .. Direct Squadron activities and personnel; $1.5 million assets.
- .. Airfield operations; tower, approach control (radar), high speed jet refueling, arresting and catapult gear, fire fighting.
- .. Motor transport responsibilities: operations and repair facility for 120 vehicles (transport, refueler trucks, fire engines, construction equipment); all maintenance up to engine overhaul.

Achievements:
- .. Saved $85,000 in catapult operating funds in one year.
- .. Reduced disciplinary problems by over 50%.
- .. Reduced inoperable vehicles by 40%.

(1967-1968)
Location: Marine Wing Equipment and Repair Squadron, Vietnam

Position: Commanding Officer (Lt. Colonel)

(1965-1967)
Location: 9th Marine Corps District Headquarters, Kansas City, Missouri

Position: Assistant Director for Personnel Recruitment (Major)

(1964-1965)
Location: U.S.M.C. Command and Staff College

Position: Student (Major)

(1961-1964)
Location: Naval Air Training Command

Position: Student Control, Flight Instructor (Major, Captain)

(1955-1961)
Location: U.S.M.C. Transport Squadrons

Positions: Instructor, Operations Assistant, Flight Crew Scheduler

SALARY   Open to discussion depending on position and potential.

LOCATE   Willing to relocate.

AVAILABILITY   90 days' notice required.

LLOYD L. PILLSBURY, JR.

1297 Imperial Drive
Quincy, Illinois 62301
Telephone: (222) 498-2146

OBJECTIVE

Management Trainee: Sales/Operations

AREAS OF KNOWLEDGE

Administrative Responsibility, Coordination

Setting, Evaluating Objectives
Organizational Ability
Decision Making
Delegation of Authority

Management Reports
Presentations, Briefings

Communications
Correspondence

Personnel Policies

Records Maintenance

Employee Relations
Staff Supervision
Training Programs
Personnel Utilization, Motivation
Personnel Orientation, Evaluation

Conduct Meetings
Public Relations

PERSONAL

Birthdate: 2-28-47   Married, One Child
6'2"   185 lbs.   Excellent Health

EDUCATION

University of Illinois, Champaign, Illinois - 4 years
        Bachelor of Arts Degree
            Major: History   Minor: Mathematics

EDUCATIONAL HIGHLIGHTS

Mathematics
Analytical Geometry
Calculus I & II
Advanced Calculus
Differential Equations

Humanities
History
French
Literature
Meteorology
Physiology
Biology

STUDENT ACTIVITIES

Delta Chi Fraternity: Pledge Trainer; Chairman Home-
    coming Weekend; Chairman Father's Weekend;
    Chairman Mother's Weekend.
Phalanx: Professional Fraternity, Vice President

EXPERIENCE
May, 1980
May, 1969

UNITED STATES AIR FORCE

(Jan., 1980)
Feb., 1975)

Position: Captain. Aircraft Commander. Early Warning
        and Control Squadron, McClellan AFB, Calif.

Responsibilities:
-- Supervise and coordinate crew activities during extended duty assignments.
-- Responsible for the safety of 23 men and an aircraft valued at $10 million.
-- Perform as Test Pilot as occasion demanded.
-- Act as Scheduling Officer for pilots.

Achievements:
-- Cited for professionalism and leadership ability.
-- One of 5 young Captains selected for promotion to Aircraft Commander.
-- Held the SSIR security clearance, higher than Top Secret.

Reason for Change: Separated from military service after fulfilling commitment.

(May, 1972
Dec., 1972)

Position: Captain. Instructor Pilot, Viet Nam.

Responsibilities:
-- Responsible for orientation, training and evaluation of newly assigned pilots.
-- Act as Flying Safety Officer and Intelligence Officer.
-- Train, evaluate and approve all pilots in the Unit on standard flying and instrument procedures.

Achievements:
-- Devised and implemented new flying procedures that helped reduce risk of accidents and loss of equipment.
-- Increased area of responsibility for the Unit and improved intelligence reporting network.
-- Initiated more effective paper handling procedures.

(Nov., 1971
May, 1972)

Position: Captain. Forward Air Controller, Viet Nam.

Responsibilities:
-- Act as on-scene Commander for Troops in enemy contact situations, and in search and rescue efforts.
-- Responsible for visual locating, marking and destruction of military targets.
-- Prepare and handle briefings.

Achievements:
-- Established, and acted as Commander of Forward Communications Center.
-- Provided leadership and supervision to 15 men.
-- Acted as Unit Operations Officer; prepared daily schedule.
-- Awarded Distinguished Flying Cross for action against enemy.

(May, 1970
Nov., 1971)

Position: 1st Lieutenant. Co-Pilot, Otis Air Force Base,
Massachusetts

Responsibilities and Achievements:
-- Act as 2nd in command of crew of 15 during air-
borne missions.
-- Act as Security Officer and Central Base Property
Officer.
-- Devised a new recording system which provided
improved security for classified material; personally
responsible for several thousand dollars in office
property.

(May, 1969
May, 1970)

Position: 2nd Lieutenant. Student Pilot.

Responsibilities and Achievements:
-- Learn all aspects of flying military jet aircraft;
become academically proficient in all phases of
flying.
-- Finished 14th out of a class of 51 academically, and
16th overall.

SALARY   Negotiable in the range normal for the position.

TRAVEL   Readily agreeable to moderate travel as required.

LOCATE   Willing to relocate.

AVAILABILITY   Immediate.

REFERENCES   References available upon request.

CURRENT
MILITARY   Member, Illinois Air National Guard

INTERESTS   Reading, swimming, golf, handball.

FOREIGN   Labrador, Iceland, Viet Nam, Thailand, Korea,
TRAVEL   Philippine Islands, Guam, Japan, Okinawa, Wake Island

GERALD D. BLACK

1241 Yorktown, Halsey Village
Great Lakes, Illinois 60088
Telephone: (312) 955-6065

OBJECTIVE   <u>Administrative Assistant</u>

-- Business, Industry or Service Organization

SUMMARY   A well qualified U.S. Navy Chief Petty Officer with a background of successful performance as an administrative assistant; retiring from the Service and moving into comparable civilian work.

AREAS OF
KNOWLEDGE

Highest Level Liaison	Planning
Office Administration	Organizing
Personnel Administration	Coordinating
Problem Solving	Implementing
Training Leadership	Clerical Management
Public Relations	Correspondence
Public Speaking	Typing Skill

PERSONAL

Birthdate: 2-28-32	Married, 3 Children
5'9" 145 lbs.	Excellent Health

COMMUNITY
AND OTHER
ACTIVITIES

Parent Teachers Association - President (2 years)
Recording Secy. (1 year)
Cub Scouts - Committee Chairman (2 years)
Athletic Teams - Manager

EXPERIENCE
1950 to
Present

(1969 to
Present)

UNITED STATES NAVY

<u>Location</u>: Recruit Training Command, Naval Training
Center, Great Lakes, Illinois

<u>Position</u>: Captain's Administrative Assistant

<u>Responsibilities and Achievements</u>:
-- Carried out orders of the Commanding Officer, by personal handling or by transmitting commands to staff personnel.
-- Successfully acted as liaison with parents, recruits, military and civilian dignitaries.

- Made recommendations for changes in policy, and implemented when approved.
- Handled the Captain's correspondence, either by dictation or through letter composition.
- Received the highest commendation from the Commanding Officer on professional performance, leadership ability, tact and diplomacy at all levels of command.

(1968-1969)

Position: Chief in Charge, Recruit Training Command Legal Office

Responsibilities and Achievements:
- Acted as Supervisor for all operations of the Legal Office, including the legal library.
- Prepared reports, drafted charges for courts-martial and processed all administrative discharges.
- Settled creditor-debtor problems of Navy recruits.
- Made recommendations for changes in legal procedures and policy and implemented when approved.
- Performed investigative services for personnel, administrative or legal matters.
- Personally supervised 11 clerical/secretarial subordinates.

(1966-1968)

Location: USS CANBERRA, Heavy Cruiser, 1440 men.

Position: Chief in Charge, Training and Education Office

Responsibilities and Achievements:
- As Supervisor, Training and Education Office: organized and coordinated all administrative functions of the training programs; made recommendations for changes in training procedures and policy and implemented when approved.
- As Ship's Career Counselor: spoke to groups of 25 men (over 1100 men in total) about career programs; handled individual interviews to increase ship's retention rate.

(1966)

Position: Supervisor, Ship's Office

Responsibilities and Achievements:
- Managed, coordinated and supervised all functions of the Administrative Department, including the Post Office, Print Shop, Legal Office, Public Affairs Office, Training Office, and Personnel Office.
- Senior Chief of the Administrative Division -- 45 men: handled discipline and personnel problems.

(1962-1966)   <u>Location:</u> Naval and Marine Corps Reserve Training
               Center, Port Arthur, Texas

               <u>Position:</u> Administrative Assistant to Commanding
               Officer

               <u>Responsibilities and Achievements:</u>
               -- Managed all administrative functions; initiated
                  reports and official correspondence for Command-
                  ing Officer.
               -- Instructed Naval Reservists on seamanship and
                  administrative operations.

(1958-1962)   <u>Location:</u> USS ST. PAUL, Heavy Cruiser

               <u>Position:</u> Administrative Assistant to Vice-Admiral and
               Chief of Staff

               <u>Responsibilities and Achievements:</u>
               -- Assisted Flag Secretary in handling appointments,
                  seating arrangements at social affairs and all
                  activities of official and personal nature for the
                  Vice-Admiral.
               -- Transmitted orders to staff officers and handled
                  many confidential matters.

(1950-1958)   <u>Positions:</u> Advanced from enlisted recruit to Petty
               Officer in charge of Officer Personnel Section. Handled
               clerical assignments, managed correspondence and office
               procedures, and successfully handled supervision of
               others.

SALARY   Receptive to salary discussion in the $15,000 plus
                range.

TRAVEL   Agreeable to any amount normally consistent with a posi-
                tion of this nature.

LOCATE   Readily willing to relocate.

AVAILABILITY   March 1, 1981

EMPLOYER   Present employer is aware of approaching career retire-
CONTACT   ment and may be contacted at any time.

REFERENCES   Captain J. P. Smith, U. S. Navy, Commanding Officer,
                Recruit Training Command, Great Lakes, Illinois 60088
                    Phone: 312-729-1081

                Commander G. W. Rhodes, U. S. Navy, Executive Officer
                Recruit Training Command, Great Lakes, Illinois 60088
                    Phone: 312-729-7710

THOMAS M. SMITH

3201 Long Avenue
Milwaukee, Wisconsin 53216
Telephone: (414) 482-3605

OBJECTIVE

<u>Manager, Internal Sales and Office Operations,
Including Personnel</u>

SUMMARY

An experienced internal sales and office administrative
manager with an ability to organize, coordinate, and
successfully accomplish an operational assignment; particularly productive in securing the cooperation of others,
and with a clear understanding of the need for profit.

**AREAS OF
KNOWLEDGE**

Office Administration	Internal Sales Management
Staff Supervision	Customer Service
	Credit, Claims
Office Layout	
Office Equipment, Furniture	Plant Supervision
	Inventory Control
Work Flow, Surveys	
Expense Reduction	Personnel
Purchasing	Recruitment, Testing
	Employment, Training
Insurance	Group Benefits
	Credit Union
Traffic	
	Employee Relations
Plant Security, Safety	Union Contract Administration

**EXPERIENCE
1960 to
Present**

ABC MANUFACTURING COMPANY, Milwaukee, Wisc.
Manufacturing Division of ABC Corporation. Sales volume
$1-1/2 million.

**1969 to
Present)**

<u>Position:</u> Office Manager/Inside Sales

<u>Earnings:</u> $19,500 per year plus bonus

<u>Responsibilities:</u>
-- Handle internal sales management, working with
   customers, 14 sales agents and 1400 distributors
   by telephone, mail and in person.
-- Supervise billing, filing, cost of sales and inventory
   control; handle plant and office security.
-- Handle personnel for shop and office: recruiting,
   testing, training, insurance, union liaison and
   employee relations.
-- Purchase plant raw materials and office equipment.

Achievements:
  -- Effectively handled public and employee relations
     and publicity: Chamber of Commerce company
     member, house magazine editor, president of credit
     union, awards night director.
  -- Handled successful planning and supervision of major
     office and plant move; from 19,500 sq. ft. to
     40,000 sq. ft.
  -- Reduced bad debts to 1/10 of 1%; confined accounts
     receivable to 25 days.
  -- Successfully guided sales to a 300% increase while
     adding only 2 office employees.

Reason for Change: Resigned by mutual agreement due to
economic reversals requiring cutbacks in Divisional operations.

(1960-1969)   Position: Chief Clerk

                  Responsibilities:
                    -- Handle telephone sales orders, inquiries, quota-
                       tions; correspondence to distributors and sales
                       agents; supervised traffic rates, routing, claims;
                       supervised billing, inventory and credit; directed
                       plant protection, safety, maintenance.

                  Reason for Change: Promoted to Office Manager.

1953   VILLAGE RESTAURANT, Whitefish Bay, Wisconsin.
1960
                  Position: Owner and Manager

                  Earnings: $10,000 per year

                  Responsibilities and Achievements:
                    -- Direct all activities and operations of the restaurant:
                       purchasing, advertising, sales promotion, public
                       relations, accounting, taxes and permits.
                    -- Recruit, employ, train and supervise the staff.
                    -- Built sales through quality food and by personal
                       handling of customer relations.
                    -- Tripled sales volume in 5 years.

                  Reason for Change: Sold business due to long hours and
                  rising rents.

Military   U. S. ARMY TRANSPORTATION CORPS
Service
                  Rank: Major, after successive promotions from 2nd
                         Lieutenant

                  Responsibilities: Serve as Transportation Officer, Chicago
                  Quartermaster Depot, for 4th Army.

Achievements:
  -- Successfully supervised movement of the 33rd
     Division from Chicago to Tennessee; moved one
     million pounds per day.
  -- Personally managed and operated the only railroad
     in Korea, to evacuate Japanese from Seoul to
     Inchon for boat transportation to Japan.

Reason for Change: Returned to inactive duty.

PERSONAL   5' 10"
                175 lbs.   Married, Grown Children
                                            Excellent Health

EDUCATION   Knox College, Galesburg, Illinois - 3 years
                    Major: Economics
                    Minor: Business Administration
                Special Training Courses:
                    Illinois Central School of Transportation
                    Dale Carnegie Public Speaking

SALARY   Open to discussion in the current earnings range.

TRAVEL   Agreeable to the amount required by a position of this
                nature.

LOCATE   Prefer to remain in the Milwaukee area.

AVAILABILITY   Immediate.

EMPLOYER   Present employer is aware of change and may be con-
CONTACT   tacted at any time.

REFERENCES   References available immediately upon request.

WAYNE C. MORRIS

799 Forest Avenue
Hamilton, Ontario, Canada
Telephone: (519) 701-5962

OBJECTIVE	<u>Industrial Relations Director/Personnel Director</u>

-- Union Negotiations

AREAS OF
KNOWLEDGE

Labor Relations
Union Negotiations
Contract Administration

Personnel Policies; Formulate,
Implement, Administer

Recruitment and Hiring;
Executive, Administrative,
Hourly

Personnel Staff Super-
vision
Salary Administration
Benefits Administration

Corporate Training
Programs

Communications Program
Administration

PERSONAL

Birthdate: 6-5-44   Married, Two Children
6'   190 lbs.   Excellent Health

EDUCATION

Wayne University, Detroit, Michigan - 4 years
    B.S. in Commerce Degree - 1971
    Major: Business Management
Special Training: Dale Carnegie Course - Human Rela-
    tions and Effective Public Speaking

EDUCATIONAL
HIGHLIGHTS

Graduated Summa Cum Laude
Delta Epsilon Sigma: Scholastic Honor Society

PROFESSIONAL
MEMBERSHIPS

Industrial Management Club
Hamilton Manufacturers' Council

EXPERIENCE
May, 1971
to Present

PARK EQUIPMENT COMPANY, Detroit, Michigan.

(March, 1974
to Present)

<u>Position:</u> Personnel Manager: Hamilton, Ontario plant.
        Manufacturer of heavy equipment; 600
        employees; sales volume $53 million.

Responsibilities:
- -- Maintain administration of Collective Agreements with International Association of Machinists and Aerospace Workers (hourly and salaried).
- -- Control the 2nd and 3rd steps of grievance procedure.
- -- Direct the salaried non-union policies and position evaluation program.
- -- Recruit, screen, select and place hourly and salaried employees; direct the training programs.
- -- Control security, safety, suggestion system, first aid.
- -- Direct all employee benefit programs.

Achievements:
- -- Established good labor relations with both Bargaining Units; reduced number of grievances per 100 employees.
- -- Successfully averted a potential wildcat strike.
- -- Implemented corporate supervisory training program; improved quality of supervision and methods of discipline.
- -- Developed with local college a skills upgrading program for hourly workers.
- -- Published employee newsletter; improved communications.
- -- Reduced absenteeism; increased number of contributions to suggestion program; reduced lost time disability cases.

Reason to Change: Greater challenge and more responsibility.

March, 1972
March, 1974)

Position: Employee Relations Coordinator: Lansing, Michigan plant. Manufacturer of transmissions, torque converters and synchronizers. Sales volume $90 million; 2600 employee.

Responsibilities:
- -- Conduct 2nd step grievance meetings and write answers to grievances (hourly and salaried units).
- -- Handle research for negotiations with 2000-member Local of Allied Industrial Workers; participate in negotiations as observer and information source.
- -- Administer 3 pension programs and Supplemental Unemployment Benefit Plan; administer 3 insurance programs.
- -- Conduct extensive employee recreational program.

Achievements:
-- Helped to reach a 3-year Agreement with A. I. W. without a work stoppage.
-- Successfully settled many grievances, both white collar and hourly units.
-- Assisted in training all supervisors in an effective listening workshop; as a graduate assistant, helped train 20 supervisors in Dale Carnegie Human Relations/Public Speaking course.

(May, 1971
March, 1972)

Position: Assistant Personnel Manager: Kalamazoo, Michigan plant. Malleable iron foundry. 450 employees; sales volume $18 million.

Responsibilities:
-- Recruit and employ hourly workers, clerical and administrative personnel.
-- Develop and implement personnel procedures and forms.
-- Maintain records; control hourly employee turnover.
-- Administer Holiday Pay eligibility list.

Achievements:
-- Formalized and streamlined the procedure for allowing employee pension credits; reduced handling time and made information more available.
-- Devised and implemented an effective system of supervisory followup of probationary employees, before such employees became permanent.
-- Created a new employee orientation program, involving both supervisor and Personnel.

SALARY	Open to discussion depending on position and potential.
TRAVEL	Agreeable to any amount normally consistent with the position.
LOCATE	Willing to relocate.
AVAILABILITY	30 days' notice required.
EMPLOYER CONTACT	Present employer is not aware of decision to consider change and may not be contacted at this time.
REFERENCES	References available upon request.
INTERESTS	Teaching, flying, coaching baseball, golf, reading.

SAMUEL N. MILLER

1250 Maple Lane
Mt. Morris, Michigan 48501
Telephone: (313) 847-3982

OBJECTIVE   Plant/Manufacturing Management

SUMMARY   A thoroughly experienced manager with a background
in plant management and production -- with a capability
for taking full charge of a manufacturing operation and
producing a significant contribution to company profit.

AREAS OF   Plant Management   Cost Control
KNOWLEDGE   Industrial Engineering   Estimating
AND
EXPERIENCE   Production Methods
Production Standards   Labor Relations
Labor Negotiations

Production Control
Scheduling   Staff Supervision
Purchasing
Inventory Control   Hiring
Training

SPECIAL   Illinois Institute of Technology - Evening Division
TRAINING   Mathematics, Manufacturing Cost Control, Gear
Refresher Course

EXPERIENCE
Sept., 1965   MANUFACTURER OF AUTOMOTIVE COMPONENTS,
to Present   Flint, Michigan area.

Position: Manager of Manufacturing

Earnings: $41,000 per year

Responsibilities:
-- Exercise management control and direction of all
manufacturing and plant functions.
-- Direct Production Control, Purchasing, Inventory
Control and Scheduling.
-- Responsible for Receiving, Shipping and Stores.
-- Handle Personnel, Plant Employment, Labor Rela-
tions and Union contract negotiations.

Achievements:
-- Increased production from 100 units per day (1965)
to 1000 units per day (present).

- Improved production standards in gear division permitting sales to jump from $40,000 a month to $100,000 a month.
- Established effective small tool control by setting up a tool crib and maintenance program.
- Reduced indirect-to-direct labor ratio from 5 to 1 down to 20 to 1.
- Reduced materials inventory by 30%.

Reason to Change: Merger; new parent company bringing in own staff.

1958
1965

FILMOFORM, INC., Lyons, Illinois. Manufacturers of thermoformed plastic packaging.

(1964-1965)

Position: Plant Manager

Responsibilities and Achievements:
- Appointed Plant Manager in full charge of operations (heavy gage custom thermoforming).
- Turned plant around and began to operate profitably after 120 days.

Reason for Change: Accepted new position with greater earnings potential and opportunity for broadened knowledge in a different field.

(1958-1963)

Position: Assistant Plant Manager

Responsibilities:
- As Assistant Plant Manager, handle manufacturing problems in all areas as required.
- Continue duties of previous plant positions, which included: (1) Manager, Extrusion Department: (2) Plant Personnel Manager; (3) Plant Purchasing Manager; (4) Special Projects Engineer; (5) Manager of Model and Die Shops.

Achievements:
- Saved substantial sums by creating an Extrusion Department; expanded it to include a modern 4-1/2" line at 1/3 normal cost.
- Set up a Purchasing Department; consolidated purchasing, established controls and developed new suppliers.
- Established an effective production control system; production scheduling, daily reports, inventory control.
- Contributed heavily to layout for new plant.

-- Initiated production process inspection, safety program, foremanship training program.

Reason for Change: Promoted to Plant Manager to put plant on its feet and in the black.

1950
1958

BANCROFT METALS CORPORATION, Power Division, Carol Stream, Illinois. Manufacturers of cylinders, pneumatic valves and seals.

Position: Manager, Inspection and Quality Control Departments after successive promotions

Responsibilities as Manager, Inspection and Quality Control Depts.:
-- Full responsibility for final results and costs in inspection and quality control of Company products.
-- Direct supervision of final testers, tool and gage inspectors and tool grinders.
-- Continuing responsibility for all prior Departmental management positions.

Reason for Change: To enter career field of plant management.

PERSONAL

Excellent Health   Married, Grown Children
5'11"   190 lbs.

SALARY

Receptive to discussion in the general range of current earnings.

TRAVEL

Agreeable to any moderate amount required by the position.

LOCATE

Willing to relocate for the right opportunity.

AVAILABILITY

30 days' notice required.

EMPLOYER
CONTACT

Present employer is not aware of decision to consider change and may not be contacted at this time.

REFERENCES

Business references available on request.

WILLIAM E. MARSHALL
234 River Road
Providence, Rhode Island 02915
Telephone: (401) 703-6602

OBJECTIVE   Product/Brand Management

HIGHLIGHTS   * As Product Manager - Ice Cream Products
OF   -- Turned around a negative sales trend into a 15%
BACKGROUND   increase over previous year, in a 6-month
                              period.
                            -- Coordinated sales effort through an 18-man
                              sales force.
                            -- Initiated a distribution expense reduction pro-
                              gram; saved $45,000 per year.
                            -- Set up a cost reduction program on one product
                              which resulted in a $40,000 annual savings.

                    * As Product Manager - Vending
                            -- Increased sales 15% over a 2-year period.
                            -- Introduced nationally a new product line of 6
                              items; produced sales of $250,000 with incre-
                              mental profit of $75,000.
                            -- Initiated and supervised complete sales with-
                              drawal from 7-state western region; result was
                              an improved product line profit picture.

                    * As Marketing Assistant - Food Service Division
                            -- Developed an authorized brands and sizes list
                              for 185 products at 7 distribution centers, which
                              permitted effective inventory control and mini-
                              mized over-age stock.

                    * As District Sales Representative
                            -- Achieved 80% distribution on 5 new item introduc-
                              tions.
                            -- Received Company Hall of Fame Award for out-
                              standing performance in sales promotion.

AREAS OF   Marketing, Distribution   Sales Organization, Terri-
KNOWLEDGE   Forecasts, Budgets   tories, Meetings
                    New Products
                    Trend Analysis   Direct Sales
                                                                Distributors
                    Merchandising, Promotion   Mfgr. Representatives
                    Advertising Management
                    Media Evaluation   Markets: Food Service,
                                                                Vending, Industrial
                    Packaging

PERSONAL	Birthdate: 2-14-42 Single
	6'1" 170 lbs. Excellent Health

EDUCATION

Brown University, Graduate School of Business,
Providence, Rhode Island
   Current MBA candidate
Iowa State University, Iowa City, Iowa
   B.A. Degree
   Major: Marketing/Sales   Minor: Economics
Special Training:
   Sales Training, Inc. - Sales, Sales Management
   Sterling Institute - New Managers Seminar

EXPERIENCE SUMMARY

Oct., 1968
to Present

LEADING FOOD MANUFACTURER AND DISTRIBUTOR,
Boston. A Fortune 500 company. Sales volume in
excess of $500 million.

(Feb., 1973
to Present)

Position: Product Manager - Ice Cream Products

Earnings: $28,500 salary plus $2,000 bonus and profit
               sharing

Responsibilities:
-- Full responsibility for a product line of approximately $7 million in sales, with a merchandising
   budget of $125,000.
-- Manage sales, profit margin, pricing, packaging,
   advertising, new products, and merchandising.

Reason to Change: Present work no longer personally
challenging. Desire new opportunity for professional **and**
personal growth in marketing/sales oriented field.

(Nov., 1970
Feb., 1973)

Position: Product Manager - Vending

Responsibilities:
-- Full responsibility for a product line of $4 million
   in sales and a merchandising budget of $160,000.

(May, 1970
Nov., 1970)

Position: Marketing Assistant - Food Service Division

Responsibilities:
-- Prepare sales and profit analyses for an $18 million
   product group.

(Oct., 1968 May, 1970)	Position: District Sales Representative Responsibilities: -- Responsible for sales and distribution of company products in 155 retail grocery supermarkets, 5 major chain headquarters and 2 grocery wholesale distributors.
Sept., 1967 Oct., 1968	MARKET FOOD CENTERS, Des Moines, Iowa. Grocery supermarket chain. Position: Grocery Department Manager Responsibilities and Achievements: -- Manage and direct sales, inventory control, manpower, hiring, training, scheduling and floor merchandising for dry grocery department. -- Supervise 12 employees. -- Maintain and build customer relations. -- Reduced backroom store inventory by 50% with new stock ordering and shelf stocking program.
Oct., 1965 Oct., 1967	UNITED STATES ARMY Position: 1st Lieutenant, Artillery Responsibilities: -- Accountable Officer for $80 million in equipment, supplies and real estate; logistical support of 5,000 troops. -- Direct training operations for Artillery Officers. -- Supervise 300 civil service employees.
SALARY	Open to discussion, depending on position and potential.
TRAVEL	Any amount normally required by the position - up to 75%.
LOCATE	Willing to relocate.
AVAILABILITY	Minimum of 4-6 weeks' notice required.
EMPLOYER CONTACT	Present employer is not aware of decision to consider change and may not be contacted at this time.
REFERENCES	References available on request.
INTERESTS	Sailing, water skiing, camping.

JONATHAN R. CHASE

48 Pine Tree Trail
Portland, Maine 04120   Telephone (207) 303-6642

objective   ADMINISTRATIVE MANAGEMENT: TEXTILES

Production Planning, Control
Inventory Management
Purchasing
Claims (MSR Coordinator)
Customer Service

areas of   Textile Industry   Production Control
knowledge   Textile Manufacturing   Inventory Control

Knitting, Dyeing and Finishing   Production Scheduling
Packaging Machinery   Quality Control
                                  Reporting Systems
Customer Relations
Claims (MSR Coordination)   Purchasing
                                  Analysis, Projections
Staff Supervision, Training   Cost Calculations
Methods, Procedures   E.O.Q., R.O.P.

business
experience

1973   PARKER MANUFACTURING COMPANY, Portland, Me.
to   Manufacturer of textiles; sales volume $40 million.
present
              SUPERVISOR OF PRODUCTION PLANNING AND INVEN-
              TORY CONTROL

. Supervise the Production Planning and Inventory Con-
  trol Department; raw materials and finished goods for
  3 plants.
. Set up a new inventory control system including effec-
  tive controls, order points, order quantities.
. Work with Sales Department to improve production
  forecasting and planning systems and procedures.
Achievements
. Made inventory studies of basic stock; established
  E.O.Q. and R.O.P.
. Created savings through stock control; made econo-
  mical runs, prevented out of stock or overstocked
  conditions.
. Established a formal inventory reporting system.

1970
to
1972

PHOENIX MILLS, DIVISION OF COLE-DAVIS,
Indianapolis, Indiana. Manufacturer of textiles; Division
sales volume $30 million.

MSR COORDINATOR
Responsibilities
. Establish and administer the MSR procedure which
  served as a vehicle for reporting the quality of performance (poor to excellent) of products, individuals
  and departments.
. Procedure served for overall service performance
  analysis and used as basis of accounting and claims
  settlement.
. Prior to promotion to MRS Coordinator, handle
  responsibilities as a converter.
. Deal with customers extensively regarding converting
  services (knitting, dyeing and finishing).
Achievements
. As a special assignment, liquidated an unprofitable
  subsidiary. Disposed of inventory on hand and successfully resolved all disputes involving the factors.
. Initiated and implemented the MSR Department, and
  set it up to function smoothly.
. Established a realistic appraisal of potential claims;
  built excellent customer relations in reconciling
  differences.

1967
to
1970

DOW TEXTILES, DIVISION OF O.P.R. COMPANY,
Indianapolis, Indiana. Manufacturer of men's shirts and
golf shirts; sales volume $50 million.

PURCHASING AGENT AND PRODUCTION PLANNING
HEAD
Responsibilities
. Purchase all materials and components to manufac-
  ture sport shirts.
. Produce production schedules for 4 plants.
Achievements
. Made substantial savings by centralizing purchasing
  for the 4 plants.
. Set up inventory system which controlled stocks and
  prevented duplication of inventories at various plants.
. Established production planning schedules on a
  yearly, quarterly and monthly basis, for efficient
  operations in conformance with sales projections.

1964
to
1967

IMPERIAL MANUFACTURING COMPANY, Indianapolis, Indiana. Manufacturer of packaging machinery; sales volume $15 million.

PRODUCTION PLANNING ASSISTANT
Responsibilities and Achievements
. Handle machine loading, machine shop scheduling and sheet metal shop scheduling.
. Expedite purchase orders, control machine shop inventories and receive raw materials.
. Established systems, procedures and forms for management reporting which improved flow of operations and reduced costs.

education

DE PAUW UNIVERSITY, Greencastle, Indiana
B.S. Degree - 1963
    Major: Business Administration
    Minor: Education

personal

Birthdate: 10-14-38   Married
5'11"   190 lbs.   Excellent Health

salary

Open to discussion.

travel

Agreeable to amount of travel it takes to get the job done.

locate

Willing to relocate.

availability

30 days' notice required.

CAROLE TOWNSEND

1416 Briar Place
Chicago, Illinois 60657
Telephone: (312) 488-6806

OBJECTIVE

Public Relations:
        Research and/or Writing

Publication Editor/Assistant Editor

Advertising Research - Production

News Writing, Reporting

RELEVANT
EXPERIENCE

Public Relations	Page Layout and Composition
Research	Print Production
	Photography
Feature Writing	
News Writing	Teaching
	Team Teaching
Training and Staff Supervision	Remedial Instruction
	Curriculum Planning

PERSONAL

Birthdate: 3-2-47   Single
5'3"   125 lbs.   Excellent Health

EDUCATION

Southern Illinois University, Carbondale, Illinois - 4 years
        B.S. Degree in Education
        Major: English   Minor: Journalism

EDUCATIONAL
HIGHLIGHTS

English Grammar	Public Relations
Expository Writing	Public Speaking
News Writing	
Copy Editing	General Psychology
	Educational and Adolescent Psychology
Page Layout and Make-up	
Photography	American Literature
School Publications	English Literature
	World Literature

STUDENT
ACTIVITIES

Public Relations Student Society of America
        Attended 1968 National Convention; worked on convention newspaper.
Journalism Students Association
Dormitory Council
Dormitory Homecoming Chairman

EMPLOYMENT
Sept., 1969 to Present

HIGH SCHOOL, Chicago, Illinois.

<u>Position:</u> Teacher

<u>Responsibilities:</u>
- -- As Teacher: English, Journalism, Drama.
- -- As Advisor: School Yearbook and School Newspaper; in charge of student staff, editing, layout, production and distribution.

<u>Achievements:</u>
- -- Received Efficiency Award for Yearbook production from the American Yearbook Company - 1970.
- -- Wrote, produced and directed an assembly to sell the Yearbook.
- -- Directed student staff in the production of the Senior Show.
- -- Served on a Curriculum Planning Committee in the English Department.
- -- Attended a Human Relations Seminar.

<u>Reason to Change:</u> Desire new challenges and opportunities in a career which will make better use of Journalism background.

Summers, 1971, 1970, 1969

ELAINE REVELL, INC., Chicago, Illinois.
Temporary Office Service

<u>Position:</u> Typist

Summer, 1968

SEARS ROEBUCK & COMPANY, Chicago, Illinois.

<u>Position:</u> Sales Clerk

Oct., 1966 June, 1967 (Part-time during school)

UNIVERSITY PLAZA DORMITORY, Carbondale, Illinois.

<u>Position:</u> Receptionist

Summers, 1966 and 1965

MOTOROLA, INC., Chicago, Illinois.

<u>Position:</u> Clerk

TRAVEL

Readily agreeable to travel as required.

LOCATE

Prefer to remain in Chicago area.

AVAILABILITY

2-4 weeks' notice required.

EMPLOYER CONTACT

Present employer is not aware of decision to consider change and may <u>not</u> be contacted at this time.

RAYMOND E. GIBBS

9508 Homestead Road
Houston, Texas 77028
Telephone: (713) 614-2284

OBJECTIVE   Purchasing Management

AREAS OF   Production Purchasing   Purchase Contracts
KNOWLEDGE   R&D and MRO Purchasing   Computers, Equipment
                Purchasing and Materials   Test Instruments
                    Systems and Procedures
                EDP Applications   Electronic Components
                                                     Mechanical Components
                Departmental Administration
                Hiring, Training, Supervising   Medical Equipment
                                                     Tools, Dies, Fixtures
                Department Establishment   Machinery, Equipment
                Vendor Evaluation
                Value Analysis   Raw Materials: Metals,
                Inventory Control   Plastics, Castings,
                                                         Forgings

PERSONAL   Birthdate: 5-28-32   Married, Family
                6'0"   190 lbs.   Excellent Health

EDUCATION   Texas University, Austin, Texas
                    Bachelor of Science Degree - 1956

EXPERIENCE
1972 to   UNITED STATES HEARING INSTRUMENT CORPORATION,
Present   Houston, Texas. Manufacturer of hearing instruments,
                hearing aids and medical electronic equipment.

                Position: Purchasing Agent, reporting to President

                Responsibilities:
                    -- Direct total Departmental operations; supervise
                       buying, purchase contracts, tooling requirements,
                       expediting.
                    -- Hire and train personnel. Establish budgets, per-
                       sonnel requirements.
                    -- Maintain liaison with Department heads and manage-
                       ment.
                    -- Member of following committees: Production,
                       Engineering, Purchasing and Service, Product
                       Engineering, Make/Buy, Salvage.

Products purchased: wide variety of large to sub-miniature mechanical and electronic components; plastic and rubber molding; metal stampings, Swiss screw machine.

Achievements:
-- Relocated tooling: all stamping dies (72 die sets) for decorative hearing aid cases. Improved quality and delivery; accomplished an annual $65,000 cost avoidance.
-- Relocated seven plastic molds; incorporated engineering changes in four molds; accomplished an annual cost avoidance of $20,000.

Reason to Change: Company discontinuing manufacturing of all medical electronic instruments and concentrating on hearing aids. Reduced controllable dollar expenditure no longer a challenge to a purchasing professional.

1970
1972

SURE-GRIP CORPORATION, Houstin, Texas. Manufacturer of portable hand tools; electric, pneumatic, gasoline powered.

Position: Buyer

Responsibilities in Purchasing:
-- Castings: die castings, investment, sand, permanent mold castings.
-- Plastic Molding: injection, compression, blow mold.
-- Powdered metal, forgings, formed tubular metal, motor components.
-- Tooling: die casting, dies, patterns, plastic molds, stamping dies, lubricants, machinery.
-- Construction contracts (remodeling); special assignments troubleshooter; yearly contracts.

Achievements:
-- Effected 10% plus savings on purchases for the year; saved $204,000 on $1.9 million expenditures. Accomplished through strong negotiations, discreet vendor selection, relocation of tooling, yearly contracts.

Reason for Change: To return to Purchasing Management for increased earnings and professional status.

Sept., 1968
to Contract
Termination
Feb., 1970

HEALTHCO., INC., Houston, Texas. Manufacturers of electronic computerized health testing systems.

Position: Director of Procurement

Responsibilities:
  -- Establish a Purchasing Department previously
     non-existent; formulate and administer Purchas-
     ing policies, procedures and systems; hire and
     train Purchasing personnel.
  -- Purchase computers, computer terminals, inter-
     faces and associated equipment; electronic sub-
     systems; integrated circuits, semiconductors,
     printed circuit boards; display devices, printers;
     digital tape cassette recorders.
  -- Negotiate terms and conditions of contracts for the
     development of special "black boxes," sub-systems
     and products.
  -- Prepare contracts and establish sources to cus-
     tom manufacture and assemble all equipment and
     systems.

Reason for Change: Company in financial difficulty and
unable to continue active operations.

1959
1968

A-Y NUCLEAR CORPORATION, Houston, Texas. Manufacturer of nuclear instruments. $25 million sales.

Position: Assistant Purchasing Agent

Responsibilities:
  -- Administer daily departmental operations of 15
     people and $10 million expenditures: hiring,
     training, and supervising purchasing personnel
     (buyers, expediters, clerks); develop and imple-
     ment purchasing policies, procedures and systems,
     including EDP applications; insure the efficient and
     profitable purchase of over 30,000 items.
  -- Electronic components: transistors, diodes, inte-
     grated circuits, relays, motors, optical devices,
     memory planes, crystals, photo tubes.
  -- Mechanical components: raw material (metal,
     plastics, chemicals); radioactive chemicals and
     sources.

1957
1959

BONDED METALS, INC., Austin, Texas.

Position: Purchasing -- buying, expediting

SALARY

Open to discussion in the range of current earnings.

EMPLOYER
CONTACT

Present employer should not be contacted except by
mutual arrangement following commitment to hire.

George B. Topar
312 Wilson Street
Crawfordsville, Indiana 46307
Telephone: (219) 780-9296

OBJECTIVE   Sales, Leading to Sales Management

                        -- Industrial

SUMMARY   A successful, consistently effective Sales Executive --
                 fully experienced in personal selling and knowledgeable
                 in the industrial field -- with a performance record that
                 demonstrates a positive ability to increase sales.

AREAS OF   Sales   Office Procedures
KNOWLEDGE   Personal Selling to Key   Purchasing
                     Accounts   Expediting
                                                      Material Take Off
                 Customer Service
                 Complaint Investigation/   Public Relations
                     Settlement

                 Sales Supervision   Contractors
                 Territory Layout   Engineers
                 Pricing   Land Developers
                                                      Distributors
                 Specification Sales
                 Demonstrations

PERSONAL   Birthdate: 3-16-42   Married, Two Children
                 5'11"   195 lbs.   Excellent Health

EDUCATION   University of Denver, Denver, Colorado -- 1961-1964
                        Major: Business Administration

EXPERIENCE
SUMMARY
1967 to   BESSANT PIPE AND FOUNDRY COMPANY, Peoria,
Present   Illinois. Manufacturer and distributor of cast iron and
                 plastic PVC pipe and fittings for sewer and water con-
                 struction and maintenance. Sales volume $10 million.

(1970 to   Position: District Manager
Present)
                 Earnings: $21,000 per year plus car and expenses

                 Responsibilities:
                     -- Personally sell to customers, including distributors
                        and contractors.

-- Handle customer complaints, and adjust satisfactorily.
-- Supervise one additional sales representative, and arrange territorial layout.
-- Handle material take offs and specification sales.

Achievements:
-- Number one ranked salesman in Western Sales Area for last 7 years.
-- Sold up to $1.5 million per year.
-- Currently producing 2/3 of the total sales of the 3-man Western Territory.
-- Personal operating expenses held to a 4-5% yearly increase, lowest in the territory.
-- As District Manager, established a new direct territory from a previous jobber distribution and increased the territory sales 90%; set up 2 new distributors; sold 15 new customers; trained a sales representative.

Reason to Change: Seek a new challenge with greater opportunity for personal growth, development and earnings.

(1967-1970)   Position: Sales Representative

Responsibilities:
-- Handle sales to customers, especially contractors.
-- Price the bid estimates as required.
-- Handle customer and public relations, continuously building the quality image of the Company.
-- Set up office procedures where necessary.

Achievements:
-- Added 22 new accounts in 3 years.
-- Had territory increased from 2 states to 4.

Reason for Change: Promotion to District Manager.

1964
1967   NEWMARK LABORATORIES, INC., Ithica, New York. Pharmaceutical manufacturer.

Position: Sales Representative

Responsibilities:
-- Develop and manage a new territory.
-- Build sales by calls on physicians, hospitals, retailers, and wholesalers.
-- Develop creative new techniques for increasing product sales.
-- Maintain current knowledge of competitive products.

Achievements:
-- Created a good rapport and better relations with customers and prospects; improved Company image.
-- Built the Walgreen volume -- one of Company's largest accounts.
-- Had salary increased $900 within a 22-month period.
-- Helped increase Chicago territory volume from $350,000 to $400,000 in one year; 14% increase, with all products up.

Reason for Change: To enter the field of selling industrial products.

SALARY   Negotiable in the current earnings range.

TRAVEL   Agreeable to the amount required by the position.

LOCATE   Willing to relocate, depending on location and potential.

AVAILABILITY   30 days' notice required.

EMPLOYER   Present employer is not aware of decision to consider
CONTACT   change and may not be contacted at this time.

REFERENCES   References are available upon request.

INTERESTS   Camping, outdoor sports, gardening, scale model
                construction.

COMMUNITY   Church Activities
SERVICE   Independent Order of Foresters
                Boy Scouts of America: Scoutmaster and Senior Scout
                    Advisor

ROBERT P. GRAVES
6030 North Sheridan Road
Chicago, Illinois 60626
Telephone: (312) 526-3304

OBJECTIVE	<u>Sales/Marketing Management</u>

SUMMARY

A capable, productive Sales Executive -- knowledgeable and experienced -- combining high volume personal selling of major accounts with an administrative ability that multiplies sales through the stimulation of the sales force.

AREAS OF
KNOWLEDGE
AND
EXPERIENCE

Sales Administration	Sales Hiring, Training
Policy Determination	Sales Supervision, Motivation
Sales Forecasting	
	Territory Layout
Personal Selling of Key	Compensation Plans
Accounts	Quota Development
Customer Relations	
	Industrial Sales
Distribution	Use and OEM
Marketing	Automotive Redistribution
Merchandising	Hardware
Sales Promotion	Premium and Incentive
Product Line Development	Mass Merchandising
Sales Meetings	Distributors, Wholesalers
Trade Shows	Manufacturers Representatives

PERSONAL

Birthdate: 9-10-37	Married, Family
5'9" 175 lbs.	Excellent Health

EDUCATION

Carleton College, Northfield, Minnesota
   B.A. Degree - Business Administration
   Major: Management

Special Study:
   American Management Association Seminars
   University of Wisconsin Seminars

PROFESSIONAL
MEMBERSHIPS

National Association of Market Developers
American Society of Tool Engineers
Sales and Marketing Executive Association of Chicago

JONES INDUSTRIES, INC., San Francisco, California.
Subsidiary of ABC Company, New York, New York. Leading maker of hand tools. Annual volume $50 million.

Position: Regional Sales Manager, headquartering in the
Chicago area

Earnings: $29,000 salary and commission, plus bonus
and all fringes

Responsibilities:
-- Total responsibility for sales of all product lines in
all markets, in 10 midwestern states.
-- Represent six corporate divisions of the Company,
and produce sales of about $5 million annually.
-- Select, train, direct and motivate a sales force of
16 direct sales representatives and 4 manufacturers'
representative organizations in specialized fields.
-- Manage sales for direct use, OEM and redistribu-
tions through wholesalers and jobbers.
-- Direct the sales force in planned selling toward
specific goals.

Achievements:

-- In less than 5 years, increased monthly Regional
volume from $150,000 to $435,000, while maintaining proper sales/cost ratio.

-- Created a volume-building sales force of loyal, dedicated and enthusiastic men.

-- Built and maintained a solid customer/company
relationship.

Reason to Change: Because of management changes as a
result of recent merger, potential for future personal
growth and advancement greatly reduced.

(1963-1969) Position: District Manager, Metropolitan Chicago territory

Earnings: $13,000 salary and commission

Responsibilities: Act as Field Sales Representative for
all six Divisions and all brands of the Company.

Achievements:

-- In a territory which had almost no sales in 1958,
built distribution substantially, both wholesaler and
dealer, in automotive and hardware markets.

Reason for Change: Promoted to Regional Sales Manager.

1956
1960

NATIONAL SAFETY BAG COMPANY, Chicago, Illinois.
Paper converters. Annual sales volume $3.5 million.

Position: Administrative Assistant to Sales Manager

Responsibilities:
-- Handle both internal and external areas of sales
and marketing including sales correspondence,
order desk, production printing layout, sample
production, advertising and pricing.
-- Represent the Company as Field Sales Representative, selling large paper bags, liners and covers
to the feed, seed, chemical, meat packing and milk
industries.

Achievements:

-- Promoted to Administrative Assistant from Sales
Trainee, as a result of personal effort and progress.

Reason for Change: Resigned to accept a new position
which offered much greater opportunity for personal and
business development.

SALARY

Negotiable, depending on earnings potential and other
income considerations.

TRAVEL

Agreeable to whatever amount of travel is required to
handle the position successfully.

LOCATE

Readily willing to relocate.

AVAILABILITY

Minimum of 30 days' notice required.

EMPLOYER
CONTACT

Present employer is not aware of decision to consider
change and may not be contacted at this time.

REFERENCES

References available upon request.

MRS. WILMA K. BRERMAN

7104 Palm Avenue
Chicago, Illinois 60646
Telephone: (312) 447-4115

OBJECTIVE Secretary/Executive Secretary

SUMMARY A qualified, experienced Secretary with a demonstrated capability. Knowledgeable in office administration, conventions and meetings, with a consistent record of contributions in each assignment.

BUSINESS KNOWLEDGE

Office Administration

Office Operations	Telephone Conferences
Procedures Planning	Correspondence
Staff Supervision, Training	Manuals, Files, Records

Conventions, Meetings

Planning, Execution, Procedures	Communications
Hotel Liaison	Staffing
	Security
Program Development	Transportation
Reservation Procedures	
Meeting Rooms, Protocol	Menu Planning
Business/Social Functions	

Secretarial Skills

Shorthand - 120 wpm	Figure Work
Typing - 65 wpm	Office Machines
Letter Composition	

PERSONAL

| Birthdate: 10-1-42 | Divorced |
| 5'2" | 110 lbs. | Excellent Health |

EDUCATION Central YMCA Community College, Chicago, Ill. - **2 years**
       Major: Secretarial and Office Administration
Special Training:
       Patricia Stevens Career College - Executive Secretarial Course - Evening Division: 6 months (1972)

EXPERIENCE
May, 1969
Oct., 1980

GLOBAL INSURANCE COMPANY, Chicago, Illinois.

Position: Secretary, Sales Department

Earnings: $975 per month plus bonus

Responsibilities:
- -- Handle secretarial duties with a minimum of super-vision.
- -- Maintain daily calendar for the Sales Manager.
- -- Assist in preparation of minutes of the Company sales meetings.
- -- Handle all record keeping of about 20 confidential commission agreements.
- -- Make travel and lodging reservations.
- -- Compose any necessary letters and memos; take dictation.

Reason to Change: Seek a new challenge for personal and professional growth.

May, 1966
May, 1969

TRANS AMERICA SALES CORPORATION, Chicago, Illinois. Import-export distributing firm. Annual sales $1.5 million.

Position: Secretary

Responsibilities:
- -- Provide full secretarial service to sales manager and 2 assistants: letter composition, shorthand, typing and customer handling.
- -- Maintain the personal books for principal employer; all original entries and balancing.
- -- Handle customer relations, service and complaints.

Reason for Change: Resigned to accept a better position.

1963
1965

AMERICAN ASSOCIATION OF HOME BUILDERS, Chicago, Illinois.

Position: Secretary

Responsibilities:
- -- Assist the Convention Arrangements Director in varied aspects of planning and execution of annual convention (largest closed trade show in Chicago).
- -- Handle registrations, hotel reservations and incoming money.
- -- Maintain close facilities liaison with McCormick Place, Chicago, site of the convention.
- -- Arrange for convention food and entertainment.

Reason for Change: Convention headquarters moved to Houston, Texas.

TRAVEL	Agreeable to any moderate amount of travel.
LOCATE	Willing to relocate.
AVAILABILITY	Immediate.
EMPLOYER CONTACT	Present employer is aware of change and may be contacted at any time.

> Mr. William Gordon, Sales Manager
> Global Insurance Company
> 20 North Wacker Drive
> Chicago, Illinois 60606
> Telephone: (312) 321-8630

REFERENCES	Business and personal references available upon request.
INTERESTS	Bridge, interior decorating, antiques, golf.

JON HARKINS

11528 Harvard Avenue
Cleveland, Ohio 44122
Telephone: (216) 742-8867

OBJECTIVE <u>Social Service Position</u>

-- Leading to Supervision/Administration

AREAS OF KNOWLEDGE AND WORK EXPERIENCE

<u>Social Service</u>

Criminal Investigation	Recreational Programming
Case Reporting	Group Therapy
	Community Organization
Interviewing	
Problem Identification	Volunteer Guidance
Treatment Application	Interagency Referral
Home Evaluation	Reality Therapy
Placement	
	Academic Counseling
Community Relations	Employment Counseling
Public Relations	Family Counseling

<u>General Business</u>

Employee Supervision	Personnel
Customer Relations	Employment
Sales Promotion	Training
Purchasing	Payroll

PERSONAL Birthdate: 7-18-50   Single
6'1"   195 lbs.   Excellent Health

EDUCATION Case Western Reserve University, Cleveland, Ohio
B.A. Degree - 1972
Major: Social Service
Minors: Sociology, Political Science

PROFESSIONAL ACTIVITIES National Association of Social Workers
Ohio Correctional Association
Cuyahoga County Assn. of Crime and Delinquency

EDUCATIONAL HIGHLIGHTS

<u>Social Work</u>

History of Social Welfare	Sociology
Theory of Social Work	Industrial Sociology
Social Welfare Systems	Social Psychology
Case Analysis	Introductory Psychology
Interviewing	Abnormal Psychology
Field Work -- Parole Agent	Educational Psychology

148

<u>Related Courses</u>

Political Theory   Religion
American Politics   Philosophy
Latin American Politics   Constitutional History
Urban Politics   Economics
Criminology   Statistics
American Criminal Justice
   Systems

STUDENT
ACTIVITIES

President, Residence Center
Representative, Residence Center Association
Chairman, Orientation Committee for Freshmen
Student Foundation: University Public Relations,
   University Promotion and Recruiting
Social Service Club: Volunteer for Community Youth
   Center

Assistant Producer, Midwest Variety Show Tour of
   Old Age Facilities and Hospitals
Childrens' Plays presented to Local Schools:
   Participant
Sociological Analysis of Industrial Plant

Earned 75% of college expenses.

EXPERIENCE
July, 1972
to Present

OHIO DEPARTMENT OF CORRECTIONS, Ohio Youth
Authority, Parole Division, Columbus, Ohio.

<u>Position:</u> Senior Parole Agent

<u>Responsibilities:</u>
-- Handle criminal investigations on inmates of Ohio
   Boys School and Ohio Youth Center; make home
   evaluations; prepare social histories; interview
   inmates.
-- Make social problem identification and supervise
   juveniles and young adults to age 25; counsel
   individuals and their families.
-- Prepare placement for prospective parolees; resi-
   dence, education, employment.
-- Serve on the Parole Committee for the Cleveland
   office.
-- Act as Probable Cause Hearing Officer.
-- Handle public relations for the Department of Cor-
   rections; provide the primary link between the
   Department and the community.
-- Prosecute parole violators.

Additional Activities:

-- Attended 1973 national conference of the National Association of Social Workers.
-- Participated in Seminar at National Center for Drug Research, Lexington, Kentucky (1973).
-- Managed volunteer program using college students.
-- Participant in Employer Motivation Program for jobs for parolees.
-- Participant in Community Referral Service for parolees.
-- Speaker on Law Enforcement and Corrections at schools and community organizations.

Reason for Change: Seek broader experience leading to administrative position with greater earnings.

May, 1965
Oct., 1971
(Part time
summers
full time)

A & W ROOT BEER DRIVE-IN, Cleveland, Ohio.

Position: General Manager; Cashier; Cook

Responsibilities:

-- Manage this family owned business; direct the operations; hire, train and supervise the employees.
-- Set up work schedules; handle payroll.
-- Purchase food and supplies; maintain quality of finished products; maintain equipment.

Achievements:

-- Established uniform training procedures including a manual of operations.
-- In one year, increased sales by 10%; decreased employee turnover as much as 20%.

Reason for Change: To continue college.

SALARY	Open to discussion; position itself of prime importance.
TRAVEL	Agreeable to any travel required; have car.
LOCATE	Readily willing to relocate.
AVAILABILITY	2 weeks' notice required.
EMPLOYER CONTACT	Present employer is not aware of decision to consider change and may not be contacted at this time.
REFERENCES	References available upon request.
INTERESTS	Reading, cycling, travel, sports, community activities, classical music.

SANDRA L. YOUNG

384 Wellington
Dover, Delaware 19901
Telephone: (302) 734-0581

OBJECTIVE   <u>Teacher: Elementary School (K-6)</u>

AREAS OF
KNOWLEDGE

Teaching	Parent-Teacher Relations
Tutoring	Upper Grades
Team Teaching	Student Leadership
Programmed Instruction	Extracurricular Activities
Open Education	Sports Instruction
Curriculum Development	Conducting Seminars

PERSONAL

Birthdate: 10-7-58   Single
5'7"   118 lbs.   Excellent Health

EDUCATION

Sarah Lawrence College, Bronxville, New York - 4 years
   B.S. Degree - May, 1980
      Major: Elementary Education   Minor: English

EDUCATIONAL
HIGHLIGHTS

<u>Education</u>
Foundations of Education
   (2 semesters)
The Teaching of Reading
Winter Term Education
   Course

Creative Dramatics
Student Teaching and
   Seminars
Independent Study in Educa-
   tion (teaching)

Music for Children
Educational Psychology

<u>English</u>
English Composition
The American Novel
Folklore
Salmagundi Workshop
   (literary magazine)
African Literature
The Rise of the Modern
   American Novel
Contemporary Drama

<u>French</u>
French Literature
French Poetry
Oral and Written French

STUDENT
ACTIVITIES

Dormitory President, Secretary (La Maison Francaise)
Honors List (3 semesters)
Leader of Christian Fellowship Group
Vice President, Eastern New York State Inter-Varsity
   Christian Fellowship Area Committee

"A Recycled Classroom" Project: member of team of
   5 which successfully completed the project.

TEACHING
EXPERIENCE
Student Teaching
Senior Year

JEFFERSON ELEMENTARY SCHOOL, New York City.

<u>Position:</u> Student Teacher: 4th, 5th, 6th Grades

<u>Responsibilities:</u>

<u>5th Grade</u>
.. Direct a full scale play.
.. Teach a new social studies program --MACOS.
.. Teach regular subjects.
.. Teach Individualized Programmed Math.

<u>4th Grade</u>
.. Member of teaching team.
.. Participate in open education.
.. Teach new science program (ESS).
.. Motivational teaching of underachieving (remedial) language arts group.

<u>5th and 6th Grades</u>
.. Teach new language arts "mini-course."

<u>Achievements:</u>
.. Presented a play successfully to entire school and parents.
.. Became familiar with newest teaching techniques.
.. Increased the enthusiasm and improved results on the part of underachieving group of 4th graders.

Student Teaching
Junior Year

ELEMENTARY SCHOOLS, Bronxville, New York.

<u>Position:</u> Assistant Teacher; Volunteer Teacher

<u>Responsibilities:</u>
.. Teach creative dramatics to 1st and 2nd grade combination to improve reading skills and attitude.
.. Teach creative dramatics to 5th grade to test self-concept.
.. Teach English to two French Canadian children.

WORK
EXPERIENCE
Summers
1978,1979

DON MALLORY TENNIS CAMPUS, Dover, Delaware.

<u>Position:</u> Assistant Recreation and Program Director

<u>Responsibilities:</u>
.. Give tennis instruction daily; plan all non-tennis and rainy day activities; plan social functions and trips; direct dramatic productions; supervise a dormitory.

Summers 1973-1977	CITY OF DOVER, DELAWARE

Position: Counselor-Ravine Forest Day Camp

Responsibilities:
.. Handle instruction of camp activities including archery, trampoline, nature skills, creative dramatics; lead songs at all camp meetings.

SALARY	Open to discussion; position itself of prime importance.
LOCATE	Willing to relocate.
AVAILABILITY	Immediate.
REFERENCES	References are available on request.
INTERESTS	Tennis, dramatics, Christian activities.
FOREIGN LANGUAGE	French: read, write and speak fluently.

section 7

preparing the draft of your resume

Now that you have completed the data gathering, with the essential facts at hand, you are about to start on a very important part of the resume—the writing.

Keep in mind that what you are endeavoring to do is to create a sales tool to assist in marketing a product—YOU. So, write the resume in a way to attract the attention of a prospective employer...and stimulate his interest in talking to you personally.

In general, follow the format of the sample resumes included in this Guide. Use the various item headings which apply in your personal situation. Incidentally, the myth that says resumes must be only one page in length is just that—a myth. If you strongly feel that in your case, another format or arrangement is in order, by all means use it. Keep in mind the principles of a good resume being easy to read, complete and yet brief. Remember to underscore, use all caps, and space out sections for emphasis and to separate the various sections.

Style of writing is important, to the extent of its being straightforward and unflowery. Avoid the pronoun "I" and forget long preambles or introductory statements. You must conserve the employer's time, and you do it by writing in a simple, clear and concise manner.

Your choice of words, particularly verbs, can help you. Start your sentences or statements with verbs denoting positive activity. For example, begin your "Achievement" statements with action words like: Created, Supervised, Initiated, Successfully introduced, Led, Built, Increased. Use the Positive/Action words shown at the end of this Section.

Remember to keep the format simple, the sentences short, and clearly stress the key areas.

Begin by writing a rough draft. You can start the first draft by writing from Items 1 through 5 on Page 1 of the Data Sheets, following with your work experience (except in the case of recent college students or graduates, where educational highlights are inserted prior to work experience). Conclude the draft with Items 6 through 16 on the second page of the Data Sheets, following the format of the sample resumes.

Before making your final draft, run down the following check list.

In the light of the direct, pertinent questions about YOU which follow, be objective and see how you have done in your resume.

Can you spot any omissions? Any points in your resume effort where you could make improvement?

1. Have you taken enough time to really write your resume as well as you can?

2. Is it written through the eyes of the employer? Will he want to see you because of

how you have pictured yourself? Have you shown how you contributed to the success of your past employers?

3. Is the length of the resume 3 typed pages or less? A man's legs, Abraham Lincoln is quoted as saying, should be just long enough to reach the ground. Your resume should be long enough to do the job . . . and no longer.

4. Does it look uncrowded on the pages? Plenty of "white space"?

5. Spelling and grammar in good shape?

6. Have you avoided all exaggerations, so that you can support or document each statement? You must *not* appear to be egotistical.

7. Did you stick with short paragraphs and concise statements?

8. Is your OBJECTIVE clearly and simply stated?

9. Does your resume contain only pertinent material, with all extraneous matter removed?

10. Did you keep the tone positive all the way through?

11. Are your *Achievements* listed in order of importance, from the employer's viewpoint?

12. Reread your Reasons for Change; are they reasonable? Did you avoid putting a former employer in a bad light?

13. In describing a past employer's activities and sales volume, have you shown any private company data which should be kept confidential?

14. Is your salary requirement reasonable, practicable and attainable? Would it be better to show it open to discussion?

15. Under *Travel* and *Locate,* have you eliminated any statements about what you won't do? It's better to state what you are willing to do.

16. Under *Availability,* are you willing to give your present company, if you are employed, adequate and reasonable notice?

Now, type your resume letter-perfect and camera-ready for printing. Here is where *quality* reproduction begins. So use a good clean typeface, preferably larger than "elite." Remember to make the resume easy to read, because it's a SALES TOOL. Allow good margins for readability, top, bottom and sides.

Finally, proofread the typed copy once more . . . it will be well worth it to guarantee avoiding grammatical and typographical errors, wrong zip codes and wrong phone numbers.

Positive/Action Words for Resume Preparation

Capacity
Capability
Ability
Competence
Effectiveness
Maturity

Management
Administrative
Technical
Executive

Professional
Academic

Successful
Capable
Competent
Qualified
Proficient
Efficient
Consistent
Knowledgeable
Experienced
Productive
Effective
Mature
Stable
Well-educated

Versatile
Well-rounded
Scope
Wide background
Resourceful
Equipped

Significantly
Substantially
Repeatedly

Designed
Developed
Built
Established
Implemented
Controlled
Guided

Managed
Directed
Supervised

Initiated
Created
Organized

Trained
Led
Coordinated

Improved
Expanded

Achieved
Accomplished
Effected

Thoroughly
Completely
Particularly
Preference
Pertinent

Thorough
Sound
Complete
Positive
Vigorous
Profitable

Evident
Demonstrated
Proven

Major
Significant
Responsible
Consistent
Contributions
Substantial

Potential

Specialist

Performance

Record

Increasing
Expanding
Enlarging
Building
Developing

Increased
Instituted
Introduced
Arranged
Installed

Eliminated
Saved
Reduced
Prevented

Recruited
Trained

section 8

printing the resume

Quality

Uppermost is the matter of quality in the resume reproduction. There is just no substitute. Remember, the resume is YOU when you aren't there. Just as you would want to appear your best for an interview, so have your resume reproduced well, so it can represent you at the very best level.

Method of Reproduction

The major ingredient in the printing aspect of resume preparation is simply this: buy the best printing you can afford . . . and use a fine quality paper stock.

The desired printing *method* is offset, sometimes referred to as multilith. A quality offset job is generally superior to a typical Xerox or similar reproduction. However, a *poor* printing job, by any method, results in a poor appearing resume.

The so-called "planograph" method is actually offset, but often is not of the finest quality and is frequently run on the least expensive paper.

Mimeograph reproduction is not used to any great extent, having been supplanted by offset printing. First class mimeo reproduction is hard to get. If you do get it, it is an acceptable method of reproduction, but still not the equal of quality offset.

Quantity

Plan carefully for the number of copies you feel you will reasonably need . . . and add a few more for reserve. In printing, by any method, the additional cost of running 50 as compared to 25, or of running 100 copies as compared to 50, is very small.

Costs

You can expect to pay from $4 to $6 per 100 copies per page for printing your resumes, plus the extra cost of special paper if you use the finest quality. These prices do *not* include the cost of having your resume typed, in perfect fashion, so that each page is camera-ready.

Typing costs vary, but will run $1.50 to $2 per page. Insist on a good clear type, and error-free work.

If one to three copies only are required, then get the best Xerox copies you can. It is not necessary for resumes to be individually typed, but you should *not* use carbon copies.

Paper

Paper stock normally supplied by a printer is 20 pound No. 4 Sulfite bond. Do not use a 16 pound stock or any lower quality paper.

For fine results, use a 20 pound, 25% cotton content bond. The very best paper is a 24 pound, 25% cotton content bond. It is not necessary to use a 50% or 100% cotton content paper.

If you use the mimeograph method, then a good 20 pound or 24 pound mimeograph bond should be specified.

Gathering and Stapling

Resumes of more than one page, and most will run two or three pages, should be gathered, and stapled with one staple in the upper left-hand corner. Colored backing sheets are not necessary.

Photograph

Very few resumes contain a photo for the simple reason that a potential employer is much more interested in what you have *done*, or what he *thinks* you can do for him, than he is in what you look like. Further, since many photos tend to be flattering, it's hard to actually look as good, in person, as your photo may suggest. So, since it is *not* necessary, why include it?

If you do decide to use a photo, you should provide a good glossy print of yourself to a company that specializes in quantity prints. Order 50 or 100 prints measuring about 1 ¼" x 1 ½" and affix a print to the first page of each resume, usually in one of the upper corners of the page. Cost is $7 to $10. If you prefer, your offset printer can use a separate plate and run a 100-screen print right on your resume itself. Cost may be $10 extra. But, good quality is hard to get.

Final Printing

Print each page of your resume on a separate sheet of paper. Use one side only.

section 9

how to use your resume

Your personal, individual resume is YOUR sales tool. By itself, it will not get you a position . . . but it will open doors for you, will make it possible for you to introduce yourself to prospective employers. It will enable you to answer want ads, and permit personal and business contacts and friends of yours to help you market yourself.

Position Search Program

It is best to lay out a comprehensive and aggressive campaign to cover all aspects of the position search. If you have someone to advise you, or review the plan, so much the better provided the individual is capable of being objective and has had experience as an employer. Placement directors of graduate schools of business are usually very capable individuals and experienced in the job market. Bank officers often have a good knowledge of the market in the individual community. What you need is maximum exposure to the openings which exist, and which are appropriate for you.

Once you have established a plan, then follow it diligently, with perseverance and effort. It can take 30 days or 3-6 months or more, depending on many factors.

Want Ads

Watch for the ad possibilities in the leading newspaper of your community, and the leading paper in your nearest large metropolitan city . . . or read the best papers from any area to which you are willing to relocate.

Always send a cover letter with your resume. See the samples and suggestions provided in the Guide.

Employers Direct

You may want to select a number of companies for whom you feel you could contribute, and who might have openings in which you would be interested. Refer to the list of leading reference books at the end of this Guide, available to you in public libraries.

As in the case of answering ads, always send a cover letter. Wherever possible, address your letter to an individual in the company, by name and title. It ideally should be a person who can make the decision to employ you.

Refer to one of the sample letters which you can modify to fit your circumstances. In any letter you write, be yourself! Be conservative, but be positive in your approach.

Business and Personal Contacts

Do not call or write these people with the thought that they can hire you themselves. But rather see if they can *refer* you to someone they know, who might have an opening or could otherwise be helpful.

Send your resume, along with a note explaining what you are asking them to do to assist you.

Employment Agencies

If you choose to work with agencies, then select only the best . . . from the standpoint of their being honest, capable and *able* to be of assistance. Do not make a blanket resume mailing to a large number of unknown agencies. Study any contract carefully before signing.

Executive Recruiters, Management Consultants and Others

You may want to consider writing to executive recruiters, management consulting firms who recruit, the Big 8 accounting firms and leading metropolitan banks. These organizations, directly or indirectly, are always on the lookout for outstanding executives.

However, keep in mind that such firms are seeking people, in a broad range of functions, areas and industries, usually on assignment from their employer clients. Naturally, they search for the best qualified people, based on education, experience and success in their jobs.

To be considered by these firms, then, you must have a top quality resume, a well written cover letter, an exceptionally good earnings record, and you must be a particularly capable individual. Your past and current earnings should be above the $25,000 figure. Recruiters prefer to deal with executives currently employed.

If you plan a mailing to this group, see the list of better quality firms shown at the end of the Guide. Add additional names of leading recruiters and consultants in your own area.

School, College and Association Placement Services

Business schools, vocational schools, junior colleges, community colleges, four-year colleges and universities almost always maintain a placement service. While you should not rely *only* on such placement service for your new position, you should make full use of this source. Depending on your particular school, it can be a very good source for you, if you are either a current student or an alumnus.

Professional associations, business and trade associations often maintain placement services for their members. Make sure that your present employer doesn't receive a copy of your resume!

Executive Clearing Houses

Basically, these firms are exactly what this heading suggests. The idea is for both employers and candidates to provide input into a retrieval system usually computerized. It is a method of bringing information about employers and applicants to each other, in a confidential manner.

As an applicant or candidate, you will be expected to share the cost of the service.

Executive Career Counselors

These firms, known as Career Counselors or Executive Guidance companies, almost always charge substantial fees which are paid by the individual using the service. These companies cannot normally guarantee employment, although they may suggest the high probability. Fees are not contingent upon employment but rather on general or specific services.

Some of these firms include psychological appraisals as a major selling point. An individual over 40 years old with ten to fifteen years in a career may want to question the value of this. Even if a career change is indicated, making the switch may not be likely or possible.

Other firms use a technique of depth-interviewing to assist the individual in developing materials by which he can show how his talents and experience enable him to meet an employer's needs and solve his problems. While such a portfolio may have considerable value to an individual, in forcing him to review his career highlights, he must still find a way to get before an employer to use it.

As with any business or personal problem, an individual should exercise great care in selecting a counselor.

Federal Government Employment

Do you want to consider going to work for the U.S. Government? If so, you will need to find out how to go about it, the positions available, the procedures. The approaches to a government job are more formalized, and differ substanially from those used in private industry.

The Civil Service Commission governs most Federal civilian jobs, which means that you compete with other people applying for these jobs. The Commission evaluates the applicants under set rules. Certain specific occupations and some U.S. agencies, discussed below, are excepted from Civil Service Commission procedures.

Your first step, for a position under Civil Service, is to find and contact your local or nearest Federal Job Information Center. Over 100 such Centers are located across the country. They are listed under "U.S. Government" in metropolitan area phone directories. You can dial 800-555-1212 for the toll-free number of a FJIC in your state. Talk to a counselor on the phone, or better yet, go in person to the Center. All kinds of information is available to you. A preliminary step might be to phone and request copies of pamphlet BRE-37 "Working for the USA," pamphlet BRE-9 "Directory of Federal Job Information Centers" and pamphlet AN-2500 "List of Current Federal Salaries."

If you call or write a Center, do your homework first. Be prepared to tell the counselor (1) the level of education you have completed and the amount of paid and unpaid experience you have; (2) the kind of work you want; (3) the geographical areas where you want to work; (4) the lowest salary you will accept; (5) whether you are entitled to veteran preference. The counselor will know whether applications are being accepted in your chosen area for the kind of work you want. Ask the counselor to send you qualifications information and forms.

After you file a completed application, a written test may be necessary. It is required for general administrative and clerical jobs. Your test is rated, and you are placed on a list if qualified, according to your score. Remember, going to work is not automatic. There may be no need for your individual skills/experience at a particular time. Further, Federal hiring officials fill jobs in several ways. They may promote a present employee; they may hire a person who wants to transfer from another agency; they may request names of applicants from a Civil Service Commission list. Finally, assuming that you are one of the top three names on the list, they can elect to offer the job to any one of the three, and not necessarily to the highest rated.

If you are offered a job under Civil Service, your appointment can be temporary (one year or less), term (one year to less than 4 years), career-conditional or career. Normally, these are four progressive steps. You may be hired on a full time or part time basis. White collar jobs usually operate under the General Schedule (GS) pay system, with jobs being graded by degree of difficulty from GS1 to GS18. Government policy is that salaries of Federal employees should be comparable with those paid by private employers for work of the same difficulty and responsibility.

The United States Government has certain establishments with positions outside the competitive Civil Service system. The Civil Service Commission does not accept applications for these excepted positions, which include the U.S. Postal Service, agencies which are international in scope, and various others. CSC form 2421 lists these excepted organizations. Also, certain occupations, such as attorneys. In these situations, you must apply directly to the agency involved.

The U.S. Department of Labor publishes two helpful books; "Dictionary of Occupational Titles" and "Occupational Outlook Handbook." Both are for sale by the Superintendent of Documents, U.S. Government Printing Office, Washington, D.C. 20402.

Planning To Get The Right Job

Any job search can be a difficult, trying matter, if you are unprepared for it. But, being prepared for the problem, knowing how to determine the best position for yourself, how to look and where to look all ease the burden. Who do you count on to make a job search successful? You count on YOU. Nobody else cares as much about this effort as you do. Nobody will do as much as you can. Nobody can represent you like you can. Realize that you do have useful knowledge and job skills. Know that at all times, jobs are available.

Analyze yourself. List your accomplishments, personal, career, leadership. Determine your unique skills, your special abilities in teaching, selling, persuasion, mechanical and analytical. Reflect on your ease in relating to others, your community and volunteer experience. From all this self-study, can you come up with an objective that is not only right but best for you? You need to know what you have to sell; then plan how to sell it.

Now you need to structure your sales efforts (in letters, interviews, with those who can help you) toward that objective. Live it, breathe it, think of nothing else. Don't think and talk about jobs you've had. Rather, dwell on problems you have solved, quality work you have done in certain areas. Think of specific actions you took or recommended which brought good results.

Which employers need your contribution? Build a mailing list of those organizations you feel may need you and where you want to be, based on your "one best job" objective. Talk to trustworthy, knowledgeable people about their contacts. Keep building your lead list.

In your mail campaign, be persistent. Get leads, which can result in interviews, which can result in a job. Always stress what you can do for them, not what you want. Remail a list in 3-4 weeks, because time changes an organization's circumstances, and new needs arise.

Your letter to potential employers must sell you and your objective. Open with an attention getter of interest to the reader. Justify your statement. Give an example, but be brief. Demonstrate, don't just tell. Ask for an interview. Be aggressive and not passive. A practical tip: deposit all letters in the post office so that they arrive in the middle of the week.

section 10

cover letters

A transmittal or cover letter is a must with each resume you mail. For best results, direct the letter to an individual, by name and title. If this is not feasible, send your letter to a title, such as President, Vice President R&D, Controller, Sales Manager, etc., preferably to one rank or more above the position you seek. Each letter *must* be individually or automatically typed. It should never be printed or otherwise duplicated. Print a resume . . . do *not* print a cover letter.

One common mistake is to address your cover letter to a company President, on the basis that he is bound to be interested in you, that he has plenty of time to read all his mail, and that he automatically sends your resume on to another key executive who may be interested. This thinking is false in almost all cases. If, however, the President is the one person who can decide to hire you or not hire you, then do send your resume to him. Be sure to address your cover letter to him by name, as well as title.

The cover letter going with each resume you send out should be fairly short, easy to read, state the reason for mailing the resume, contain some "sell" for you and end with a polite statement requesting an interview. Don't forget to refer to the contribution to profit you can make in writing to a business; avoid egotistical or over-aggressive remarks.

Do *not* make the most common mistake of all . . . repeating the information given in your resume. Why make the employer waste his time? You may want to restate a point or two, or refer to an additional achievement . . . just don't repeat.

Study the following letters as samples only. Modify them to fit your own individual situation.

Sample Letters Nos. 1 thru 6   Answer to newspaper or trade paper ads.

Sample Letters Nos. 7 thru 17   Direct solicitation to an organization or company.

Sample Letter No. 18   Management consulting and executive recruiting firms.

Sample Letter No. 19   Business or personal contacts.

Sample Letter No. 20   Follow-up to Letter No. 19.

LETTER NO. 1
Answer to newspaper or
trade paper ads.

DOROTHY M. BROWN
8204 Robin Crest
Wheaton, Illinois 60187
Telephone: (312) 427-7104

_____
Date

Mr. John Jones, Controller		Box 127
ABC Company		The Wall Street Journal
P. O. Box 880	or	711 West Monroe Street
Oak Brook, Illinois 62120		Chicago, Illinois 60606

Dear Mr. Jones: Gentlemen:

Your ad for an Accountant in The Wall Street Journal on
____(date)_____ was interesting to me, and I'd like to be
considered. I have a strong interest in Accounting and want
to continue my career in that field.

My interest is backed by 8 years of solid experience as an
Accountant, preceded by 4 years of combined Accounting
and Office Management. I know that I can handle all normal
accounting requirements, and in addition, make my contribution to your net profit. My resume is enclosed in
great confidence.

May I talk with you?

Very truly yours,

Dorothy M. Brown

Enc.

RUTH A. COOPER
3801 West Avenue
Chicago, Illinois 60636
Telephone: (312) 236-5800

_____

Date

Mr. John Jones
Manager Accounting Department   Box 127
ABC Company   or   The Chicago Tribune
209 South LaSalle Street   435 North Michigan Avenue
Chicago, Illinois 60604   Chicago, Illinois 60611

Dear Mr. Jones: Gentlemen:

Your (___date___) ad in The Chicago Tribune described
your need for a (Junior Auditor) (Junior Accountant)
(Accounting Trainee). I am very interested for this could
be the opportunity I seek in the area in which I'd like to
begin my Accounting career.

My recent training at Metropolitan School of Business and
strong desire for this field of work qualify me to successfully handle such a position, and to make my contribution to
your organization. My resume is enclosed.

May I talk with you? I'll arrange to be there at your convenience.

Very truly yours,

Ruth A. Cooper

Enc.

This type of letter can be used by any trainee for an entry
position by adapting it to fit both the individual and the position.

LETTER NO. 3
Answer to newspaper or
trade paper ads.

ROBERT P. GRAVES
6030 North Sheridan Road
Chicago, Illinois 60626
Telephone: (312) 526-3304

_____
Date

Mr. John Jones, Vice President   Box 127
ABC Company   The Wall Street Journal
P. O. Box 880   or   711 West Monroe Street
Indianapolis, Indiana 46200   Chicago, Illinois 60606

Dear Mr. Jones: Gentlemen:

Your (____date____) ad in The Wall Street Journal described
your need for a Sales Manager. I am very interested for
this could be the challenge and opportunity I seek.

My substantial experience in Sales/Marketing Management
may be very valuable to you. This is what I can offer you to
help build corporate profit.

-- The ability to manage sales, build key accounts
   personally and to grasp the essential elements in
   your business.

-- Experience in developing substantial sales through
   better customer relations.

-- Intelligence and the capacity to learn.

-- The faculty to discern how my chosen work can
   favorably affect profit.

My resume is enclosed in great confidence, and I will appreciate your consideration. May I come and talk to you?

Very truly yours,

Robert P. Graves

Enc.

LETTER NO. 4
Answer to newspaper or
trade paper ads.

RICHARD A. JAMES
1308 Washington Boulevard
Schiller Park, Illinois 60176
Telephone: (312) 678-8068

_____
Date

Mr. John Jones, Vice President		Box 127
ABC Company		The Chicago Tribune
P. O. Box 760	or	435 North Michigan Avenue
Indianapolis, Indiana 46200		Chicago, Illinois 60611

Dear Mr. Jones: Gentlemen:

Your (__date__) ad in The Chicago Tribune described
your need for a _____. I am very interested
for this could be the challenge and opportunity I seek.

My educational training in the field of _____
and strong desire to enter this work for a career may
qualify me to successfully handle such a position, and to
make my contribution to your organization's goals. My
resume is enclosed.

May I have a personal interview, at your convenience?

Very truly yours,

Richard A. James

Enc.

LETTER NO. 5
Answer to newspaper or
trade paper ads.

SAMUEL N. MILLER
1250 Maple Lane
Mt. Morris, Michigan 48501
Telephone: (313) 847-3982

_____
Date

Mr. John Jones   Box CV 477
ABC Company   or   The Detroit Free Press
P. O. Box 1018   Main & Walther Streets
Detroit, Michigan 48224   Detroit, Michigan 48224

Dear Mr. Jones: Gentlemen:

Your November 5 ad in The Detroit Free Press described your
need for a (Plant Manager) (Engineer) (Plant Engineer). I do
want you to know that I actively seek the position.

My objective is not just a new personal responsibility, but
the opportunity for job satisfaction in the manufacturing,
engineering area, and in utilizing my abilities and experience to the fullest extent. The challenge of continued growth
is important to me.

I am an experienced (Plant Manager) (Engineer) (Plant Engineer),
knowledgeable in broad areas of manufacturing, engineering,
production, inspection. I use an imaginative approach to problems and can apply the necessary motivation to employees.

A copy of my resume is enclosed in great confidence. Your
consideration is appreciated, and I look forward to talking with
you.

Very truly yours,

Samuel N. Miller

Enc.

JONATHAN R. CHASE
48 Pine Tree Trail
Portland, Maine 04120
Telephone: (207) 303-6642

_____

Date

Box MKB 321
The Boston Globe
612 Boylston Street
Boston, Massachusetts 02121

Gentlemen:

Your (__date__) ad in the Boston Globe described your
need for a <u>Production Planning Supervisor</u>.

My 9 years of solid experience with two companies, in a
wide range of production supervisory responsibilities,
should permit me to contribute in your Planning and
Control areas. Here is what I can provide to help build
corporate profit.

-- An ability to relate applicable new developments to your Company's problems.

-- Experience in initiating new methods and
   procedures, and in balancing efforts between
   current and new practices.

-- A background in supervisory leadership.

-- The ability to work harmoniously with others
   at all levels.

I'm willing to travel and relocate, and salary is negotiable.
My resume is enclosed.

May I talk to you?

Very truly yours,

Jonathan R. Chase

Enc.

LETTER NO. 7
Direct solicitation to an
organization or company.

MRS. WILMA K. BRERMAN
7104 Palm Avenue
Chicago, Illinois 60646
Telephone: (312) 447-4115

Date

Mr. John Pope, Personnel Director
Smith, Jones and Smith
208 South LaSalle Street
Chicago, Illinois 60604

Dear Mr. Pope:

Does your firm have a need for an experienced, competent
secretary? I plan to make a job change from my present
company.

As you can see from the enclosed resume, my 14 years of
secretarial experience have been in the areas of sales and
convention planning. My former employers include an
insurance company, import-export firm, and a trade
association.

Mr. Pope, my skills are top level and I'm used to doing a
competent job for an employer. I'm available on two weeks'
notice.

May I expect a call from you so that we might talk?

Very truly yours,

Wilma K. Brerman

Enc.

LETTER NO. 8
Direct solicitation to an
organization or company.

DOROTHY M. BROWN
8204 Robin Crest
Wheaton, Illinois 60187
Telephone: (312) 427-7104

_____

Date

Mr. John W. Sommers
Manager, Accounting Department
ABC Company
4th and Jackson Streets
Chicago, Illinois 60611

Dear Mr. Sommers:

Is there a need for a young woman Accountant who can take
responsibility and produce results as part of your Accounting team?

If an area of your operation is proving too costly or is in
need of a fresh new approach, you will be interested in what
I could provide in assistance. My resume is enclosed in
confidence.

These are the things I can offer to you:

-- The ability to establish or improve Accounting
   procedures, and to grasp the essential elements
   in your business.

-- Experience in saving money through better
   analysis and sounder control of costs.

-- The faculty to discern how my chosen work can
   favorably affect your profit.

I seek a position of interest in the Accounting area, either
working on individual assignments or in a supervisory capacity.
I would expect to make my contribution to the effective operation of your Department.

May I come and see you, at your convenience?

Very truly yours,

Dorothy M. Brown

Enc.

LETTER NO. 9
Direct solicitation to an
organization or company.

DONALD S. BURDETTE
342 West Bonn Street
St. Louis, Missouri 63100

_____
Date

Mr. John W. Jones, Personnel Director
ABC Company
4th and Jackson Streets
Springfield, Illinois 62700

Dear Mr. Jones:

For the past two years I have been studying computer programming and all aspects of data processing at (_name of_
school). I'm about to graduate and am searching
for employment where a challenging opportunity may exist
in my career field.

May I come and talk with you for a few minutes? If there
is a need where you think I might fit, I believe I can assure
you of my value. My resume is enclosed.

I look forward to your reply.

Very truly yours,

Donald S. Burdette

Enc.

LETTER NO. 10
Direct solicitation to an
organization or company.

EUGENE S. ELLMAN
146 West Laurel Place
Shaker Heights, Ohio 44120
Telephone: (216) 383-9761

_____
Date

Mr. John W. Jones, President
ABC Company
910 South Stafford
Akron, Ohio 44321

Dear Mr. Jones:

Can your organization use a capable Plant Engineer or Chief
Engineer who can handle varied assignments for you in the
areas of Manufacturing Management, Production or Engineering?

I've had over 19 years of solid background in manufacturing
and engineering. I'm experienced in all plant engineering
requirements and in the construction of production machinery.
I can direct others effectively, in addition to my personal
engineering capacity.

Among my accomplishments, areas of knowledge and personal
activities are these:

-- Successfully handled varied assignments, including
creating special cutting tools that created new sales
for the Company.

-- Personally developed a number of unique and effective processes and machines which saved substantial production costs.

-- Have a demonstrated ability to work with and through
others ... and get the job done.

Salary is negotiable. I'm willing to travel and would relocate for
the right opportunity. My resume is enclosed in the greatest
confidence. May I talk with you?

Very truly yours,

Enc.

Eugene S. Ellman

LETTER NO. 11
Direct solicitation to an
organization or company.

ROBERT P. GRAVES
6030 North Sheridan Road
Chicago, Illinois 60626
Telephone: (312) 526-3304

_____
Date

Mr. John W. Jones, President
ABC Company
4th and Jackson Streets
Chicago, Illinois 60611

Dear Mr. Jones:

Can your organization use a capable sales and management
executive who can handle varied assignments for your top
management team in the areas of Sales or Marketing Management?

I've had a solid experience with a leading manufacturer of
hand tools. I'm experienced in sales administration, personnel handling and general business management. I direct
others effectively.

This is what I can offer you to help build corporate profit:

> The ability to manage sales, build key accounts
> personally and to grasp the essential elements in
> your business.

> Experience in developing substantial sales through
> better customer relations.

> Have a proven ability to set up and control dealers ...
> and get the job done.

Mr. Jones, I feel certain that I can provide the kind of sales
leadership which will help ABC products get a better share of
the market. My resume is enclosed in great confidence.

May I come and talk with you?

Very truly yours,

Robert P. Graves

Enc.

LETTER NO. 12
Direct solicitation to an
organization or company.

RICHARD A. JAMES
1308 Washington Boulevard
Schiller Park, Illinois 60176
Telephone: (312) 678-8068

_____
Date

Mr. W. P. Ruggles, Vice-President Finance
Interstate Manufacturing Corporation
111 West Monroe Street
Chicago, Illinois 60606

Dear Mr. Ruggles:

Will there be a need in your firm for a young Management
Trainee who will offer you a sound educational background
(MBA Degree in June, 1981) and a willingness to work hard?

My objective is not just a position responsibility, but the
opportunity for job satisfaction in utilizing my abilities and
educational training to the fullest extent. Finance and
Accounting are areas where I might best contribute to your
firm, because of my strong interest in these fields.

May I come in and chat with you or another executive of your
firm? If there is a need where you think I might fit, I believe
I can assure you of my value. My resume is enclosed, and
I'll be available in June, 1981, upon graduation.

I look forward to your reply.

Very truly yours,

Richard A. James

Enc.

LETTER NO. 13
Direct solicitation to an
organization or company.

ANDREW L. KENNEDY
6902 Elm Park Lane
Omaha, Nebraska 68501
Telephone: (402) 832-4216

_____
Date

Mr. John Jones, Owner
Northwest Buick Sales
418 South Kearney Avenue
Omaha, Nebraska 68523

Dear Mr. Jones:

Is there a need in your shop for a capable, well-trained
Assistant Service Manager or Head Mechanic?

My substantial experience as an auto mechanic and in
supervision may be of help to you. This is what I can offer
you to help you build your service department profit.

-- The ability to establish or improve Service
   Department practices and procedures which
   contribute to profit.

-- Experience in building inside sales and repeat
   business through better customer relations.

-- The capacity to quickly adapt myself.

My resume is enclosed. May I talk to you?

Very truly yours,

Andrew L. Kennedy

Enc.

LETTER NO. 14
Direct solicitation to an
organization or company.

THOMAS M. SMITH
3201 Long Avenue
Milwaukee, Wisconsin 53216
Telephone: (414) 482-3605

_____
Date

Mr. John Jones, Vice President
Paperboard Products Company
P. O. Box 760
Racine, Wisconsin 53401

Dear Mr. Jones:

For the past 15 years I've been engaged in internal sales
and office management supervision for a small manufacturing and distribution organization, and doing it successfully
too. But current economic conditions are causing extreme
cut-backs for our Division.

My prime motivation is to exercise my abilities and use my
accumulated experience to the fullest extent. The challenge
of continued personal growth ... and of contributing to
corporate profit ... is important to me. I want to become
associated with a company like yours where I'll have a
chance to grow. I know that you will keep the enclosed
resume in confidence.

May I come over to Racine and talk with you?

Very truly yours,

Thomas M. Smith

Enc.

LETTER NO. 15
Direct solicitation to an
organization or company.

JOHN W. THOMPSON
3112 Burke Avenue, Apt. 61
St. Paul, Minnesota 55105
Telephone: (612) 236-6597

_____
Date

Mr. William Smith
Director of Personnel
ABC Company
208 South LaSalle Street
Chicago, Illinois 60604

Dear Mr. Smith:

Is there a need in your organization for a young man to be
trained in Sales? A man who has a strong desire to take
responsibility and produce results?

I seek a position of interest and challenge with a sales
career potential. If you will let me talk with you, I feel
that I can assure you of my value and ability to make a
contribution. My resume is enclosed.

I look forward to word from you.

Very truly yours,

John W. Thompson

Enc.

This type of letter can be used for any trainee for an entry
position by adapting it to fit both the individual and the position.

LETTER NO. 16
Direct solicitation to an
organization or company.

GEORGE B. TOPAR
312 Wilson Street
Crawfordsville, Indiana 46307
Telephone: (219) 780-9296

_____
Date

Mr. Will Gordon, General Sales Manager
Oxnard Pipe and Tube Company
1170 South Beechwood Avenue
Indianapolis, Indiana 46203

Dear Mr. Gordon:

For the past seven years I've been engaged in selling pipe
and fittings for sewer and water construction for a Midwest
organization, and doing it successfully too. Prior to that
I sold pharmaceuticals for three years. But, as I see it,
I've gone as far as I can with my firm under their present
practices.

I'm a salesman. My prime motivation is to exercise my
abilities and use my accumulated experience to the fullest
extent. The challenge of continued growth in sales responsibilities and earnings is important to me.

I want to become a Sales Representative for a Company like
yours. I know that you will keep the enclosed resume in
confidence.

May I come and talk with you?

Very truly yours,

George B. Topar

Enc.

LETTER NO. 17
Direct solicitation to an
organization or company.

CAROLE TOWNSEND
1416 Briar Place
Chicago, Illinois 60657
Telephone: (312) 488-6806

Date

Mr. John Jones, Advertising Director
ABC Company
1612 W. Farwell
Chicago, Illinois 60626

Dear Mr. Jones:

Would your company benefit from the services of a creative,
innovative writer ... if my work resulted in sales, profits,
and a better company reputation in the community? I think
I can make that kind of a contribution.

I've used my excellent journalism background to some degree
in my work as a teacher. Now I seek a full-time opportunity
to pursue my chosen field as a career.

My experience, training and strong desire for this field of
work qualify me to successfully handle such a position.
My resume is enclosed.

Will you be willing to let me come in to chat with you for a
few minutes?

Very truly yours,

Carole Townsend

Enc.

LETTER NO. 18
Management consulting and
executive recruiting firms.

WILBUR P. DOWNING
6201 North Central Avenue
Boston, Massachusetts 02117
Telephone: (617) 528-8304

_____
Date

Director of Management Services
Executive Recruiters, Inc.
510 Park Avenue
New York, New York 10021

Dear Sir:

Successful sales/marketing management -- including complete
charge of marketing profit responsibility, and sales management -- is my profession.

If present profitability and sales volume are matters of
serious concern to a client company, you may be interested
in what I can do for their management team.

As an experienced management executive, I seek a new
challenge for applying my proven capability and business know-
how. I know the need for <u>profitable</u> corporate sales, and I
know how to achieve them through the direction of others.

My prime motivation is to exercise my abilities to the fullest
extent. The challenge of continued personal growth ... and
of building corporate sales ... is important to me. I want
to handle Sales Management, Marketing Management or Executive Sales at the corporate or divisional level for a progressive company. My resume is enclosed in great confidence.

I'll be happy to talk with you at your request.

Sincerely yours,

Wilbur P. Downing

Enc.

ROBERT P. GRAVES
6030 North Sheridan Road
Chicago, Illinois 60626
Telephone: (312) 526-3304

_____
Date

Mr. Paul Williams, Vice President
Universal Machine Products, Inc.
2607 West North Avenue
Chicago, Illinois 60621

Dear Paul:

I have made a decision to leave Jones Industries, Inc.,
after about fourteen years in Sales Management.

This is just a note to say that I will be anxious to get
established again, in my field, as soon as possible. I
enjoy the challenge, and I have demonstrated my ability
over many years in a competitive field.

A copy of my resume is enclosed, and I will be grateful
for any thoughts you may have for me or any contacts
you feel I may want to make.

Thanks, Paul. I'll look forward to hearing from you.

Very truly yours,

Robert P. Graves

Enc.

ROBERT P. GRAVES
6030 North Sheridan Road
Chicago, Illinois 60626
Telephone: (312) 526-3304

_____
Date

Mr. Paul Williams, Vice President
Universal Machine Products, Inc.
2607 West North Avenue
Chicago, Illinois 60621

Dear Paul:

As you will recall, several weeks ago I gave you my resume
when I decided to leave my present company.

Just wanted you to know that I'm not yet employed, but I
certainly want to get started again soon. I enjoy directing
others toward a goal, and I have shown my capability to take
a sales project or a Sales Division and wrap it up.

Another copy of my resume is enclosed. Do you have any
suggestions for me, or can you recommend any contacts you
feel I should make?

Thank you, Paul.

Very truly yours,

Robert P. Graves

Enc.

section 11

how to make your job search successful

You need to know what you are aiming for...so you can set your sights accordingly, and concentrate only on your objective. Moreover, an employer expects you to know what it is you seek, and he hopes to find it concisely stated in your resume.

If you have two or more possible objectives, well and good. Be sure you have each one clearly defined in your own mind.

Is there such a position, as you visualize it? Or do you need to modify your goal? Look at it from an outside point of view: is such a position possible, or probable? Remember, hoping and striving are not the same thing. You'll want to zero in on your goal . . . then go after it.

What are Your Qualifications?

One way to look at yourself in much the same way a potential employer does is to make two lists of your qualifications for the position you want. One of pluses and positives, one list of negatives. Your personal qualifications and the job requirements must fit before an employer will consider you favorably.

Why should an employer be interested in you? Can he tell from your resume what you do best? What have you done in the last two or three years to prepare yourself, or to remain competitive?

Realistic Probability and Expected Results

Your objective, whatever it is, can probably be realistic and you can expect to succeed if you are equipped to make a contribution to your potential employer's success, if your salary requirements are reasonable for that contribution, if you fit into his preferred age brackets, and if you maintain a certain degree of flexibility in your desires.

However, your expected results are always affected, favorably or otherwise, by such factors as the economic climate of the country and of a particular industry, whether the position desired is scarce or plentiful, and whether you are a unique or outstanding individual. Almost always, you will have competition for that one best job . . . either a little or a lot. But, somebody is going to succeed, and it can be you, if you are able to convince the employer.

You must be able to recognize the opportunity when it arrives. Don't jump too soon . . . but above all, don't procrastinate if all signs are go.

Market Yourself with a Plan

Your resume is your sales tool, but it must be *used* to let it do its job. Your basic plan must be to communicate with employers, so the resume can hopefully open some doors for you . . . and lead to interviews and finally a position.

What is really needed, for an effective job search, is a comprehensive plan for marketing yourself . . . and then determination, persistence and drive on your part to make the plan produce for you. Your long range purpose of this plan is to get the right job for you; the short term goal is to secure interviews.

So decide at the beginning that you are a Marketing Manager . . . with YOU as the product. Plan to answer ads, write employers direct, make use of business and personal contacts, contact good employment agencies and finally, use other sources such as school and association placement services. Refer again to Section IX for details on how to use these job sources.

A big psychological plus for you will be to build and maintain a good personal attitude and pace. Be positive! Go on the offensive! Maintain your enthusiasm, your momentum and don't get discouraged. Schedule yourself to work 4 to 5 hours a day on your job search, if you are unemployed. If employed, work 4 to 5 hours a week. You can't do your job search work after all your other personal desires are fulfilled . . . do it first!

Blow your own horn, in a modest way. Think and act like a successful person, and be self-confident. Stress your strongest qualifications. And if all this effort doesn't produce the right job, then do it again. Perhaps in the first effort the employers just did not have job openings. Timing can be a main factor of job availability. Thirty or sixty days later, circumstances may be entirely different . . . and this time in *your* favor.

How Long Does a Job Search Take?

Here are some of the factors which influence the length of time necessary for completing a search and landing the right position:

1. Economic conditions in general.
2. Economic conditions in your field.
3. Competition in your field in your geographic area.
4. Your skills, competence, experience.
5. Your resume, your letters.
6. How well you handle interviews.
7. How badly an employer needs to fill a position.
8. What appeals to an interviewer.

Your control of just these factors alone is limited to items 4, 5, and 6. In some cases, particularly with students, skills and experience may be very limited. Therefore, a good resume and good cover letters are essential, plus careful preparation for and handling of your interviews.

Job Search Tips

1. **Don't quit** your present job until you have secured a new one. You are in a stronger position if you search while still employed. It may be harder to do, may be inconvenient, but it's still strongly recommended.

2. **Act without delay**, once a job change decision has been reached. Whether you make a voluntary decision to search, or if your employer decides to terminate you for whatever reason, move into your program quickly.

   If you are separated by your Company, even with substantial termination pay, don't just relax for a few weeks or take a vacation first. Get the search underway!

3. **Maintain a good attitude**, about yourself and your employment problem. No one else bears the responsibility for a successful search but YOU. Gird yourself for an aggressive campaign and keep your thinking positive.

   It absolutely must be positive. It shows all over, so cast out all negatives. Think in terms of success. Expect the best. Dress the part. And down deep, have a solid belief in yourself and your search.

   No one else is really responsible for finding you that new job... no one but you. So accept that fact at the beginning.

4. **Be patient**, knowing that from one to three months of hard work on your part may be required to find that right job.

5. **Make a personal evaluation** of yourself. You can help yourself immensely by considering how others see you. With a sincere effort to be objective, say to yourself:

   > "What can I do best?
   > In what industry?
   > In what area have I contributed most?
   > Am I a planner or an administrator?
   > Better at leading, or following?
   > The bulk of my work experience is in what?
   > What are my talents, really?
   > My strengths, my weaknesses?"

6. **Maintain records** of all your search activities. Set up a 3 x 5 file, post the letters, replies, interviews and additional letters faithfully. As a result, you will always know what effort you have made with each company or other contact. You will also have the facts for a regular systematic follow-up.

7. **Follow up systematically** every likely possibility. Don't waste time on remote situations, but do diligently follow up your live leads. Do it often enough to show your continuing interest, but not so frequently as to irritate.

8. **Don't procrastinate** in your job search. Do the things you should do, when they should be done.

9. **Use references correctly** and they can be very helpful. Even though individual references are not listed in your resume, you need to have such a list available when

requested. First, decide *which* individuals in your past employer companies know your accomplishments best, and will give fair but favorable references. Add the business contacts, of as high a level as possible, who have done business with you or know you well. Include civic, professional or association leaders who know you and your abilities.

As a courteous business practice, and a very practical matter, be sure to clear with each such individual his willingness to be your reference. Do it by phone, by letter or with a personal visit, but do it.

Limit your list of references to about 4 or 6 at most, depending on your total job history. On your list, show the reference's name, company affiliation, title, street address, city, state, zip code, and telephone number including the area code.

10. **Think Carefully** before accepting any job offer, if you are currently employed. If you are unemployed or about to be, then economic and other factors may signal a quick acceptance of a job offer. In any event, some thought can be given to Position Change Considerations. Use the handy check list which follows for an easy-to-visualize comparison of some general factors governing your current and prospective positions.

11. **Salary negotiations are delicate.** Try to postpone the salary question until after you have sold yourself to the employer. When asked about your salary requirements, respond with some additional questions about the job. Ask if the interviewer will give you the range for the job.

For advance preparation, see if you can find out about the organization's salary policies and general pay reputation. Check the going rates in the area for the job you seek. Base your salary request on what you are worth to them. Don't underrate yourself. Try and get offers from other employers for comparison, and in bargaining for the job you really want.

12. **Wrap up your job search.** Write thank you notes to all people who have helped in any way, after you've started your new job. Make a list of the mistakes you made, for future reference, plus the good moves you made. Keep copies of the successful letters you used.

The Job Market

How often, when you are searching for employment, do you ask someone: "How's the job market?" Too often, probably, because it's the wrong question. You do not need an expert to tell you that when economic conditions are poor, or trending down, that the so-called job market is tight. You know that simple truth. The correct questions to ask yourself are first: "What are the current prospects in my own field of interests, training and experience?" and second, "How can I proceed to effectively create an employer's interest in me as a person and as a contributor to his goals?" Your personal job objectives and search methods are your prime considerations. Concentrate on them only.

Job Change/Career Move/Occupational Change

These three terms are not synonymous. Ask yourself: "Am I simply changing jobs, doing almost exactly what I do for my current employer, only for a new employer?" "Am I making an upward or lateral move in my planned career toward an eventual goal?" "Am I making an occupational change, with an entirely new line of work, toward a new interest or with an ultimate goal in a new field?" Think carefully before you answer.

The question that needs an answer is: "Do I have a good reason to quit?" Considering your goals (money, position, happiness), are they attainable where you now are? Readily attainable? High or low probability? Would the family need to relocate?

It's probably easiest to just change jobs. Is this what you want, what you'll be happiest with? Under some normal situations, you may really have no choice. Economic conditions, family needs, an age factor can all mitigate toward simply changing jobs. Many times, it is the one best thing to do, especially if your nature and abilities have given you a fair share of job satisfaction, earnings and family happiness.

All the basic recommendations of the GUIDE apply to a job change effort. You do need a good resume, so make it the best. You do need a well organized marketing plan, tailored just for you. You need to come across in an interview, as a highly desirable person.

Let's assume that you now have an occupation, or you're in a career, whether planned or by your development in this field of endeavor. Is an employment change desirable at this time and is the step an upward move or a lateral change? Are there growth possibilities where you are now? Would two or more years in the present organization be equally desirable to changing employers?

If you conclude that additional time in your present position will not expand your responsibilities, will not provide new training, will not permit any more growth, then why wait? Career-wise, perhaps it's time to move on. If so, plan with care, implement your search quietly but vigorously. When the new position is secured and locked up, then resign.

Is it time to change your field of work? A desire to live in another area of the country could mean a new field. While it may be possible, is success in your search probable? Do you have the funds to support yourself and your family for an interim period? Can you get the training needed in a reasonable time and without excessive cost? In a specific geographical area, do employment conditions in a new field justify the effort? Does your nature permit learning new skills and techniques easily?

In changing occupations, frequently more or different education is required, separate from training. Such activity may necessitate time away from home and family. Few people can afford to quit a regular job and re-enter school on a full time basis. So, it can mean many months of schooling, one or two evenings a week. And, hours of study at home. Are you willing to pay this price? Do you have the full family backing and support you will certainly need? Perhaps most essential, do you have the personal initiative and determination to stick with your decision? If your answer is a resounding YES, then drive ahead!

Before An Executive Changes Jobs

Because the principles are basically the same a manager or executive changing positions will want to follow the ground rules for a good resume and a successful search laid out in this GUIDE. But there are some phases of the matter which need emphasis. For example, in any labor market, a well thought out and carefully executed plan is necessary. Yet in many cases, the job hunt, which can affect every facet of an individual's career, earnings and satisfaction, is approached head-long by executives. Getting the right job for you requires a plan, the right attitude, skills, abilities and plenty of persistence.

Executives, by the nature of their work, are expected to be able to plan, organize and direct others to accomplish the goals of their own job. Shouldn't these same results-oriented methods be used in their own job searches?

Know your product—which is you. Determine, as any marketing manager would, what your personal market is. Where is it? What experience or skills pay premium rates? What does my market pay today? Are you pricing yourself realistically, considering all factors? Have you put the package (you) together well? Does your care show in your resume, in how you handle interviews, in how you relate and even in how you dress?

Have you settled on some essential goals, such as job function, security or stepping stone, size of organization, pay range? Have you built a master list (up to 50 or more) names of contacts who could help you? These are not potential employers—these are contacts who might contribute with advice or set you up for interviews with others. Now, the other master list; 50 to 200 potential employers whom you have selected as your prime targets.

Are you fully prepared for interviews? This is where the hiring action is. The more you know about each prospective employer, the better. Especially his problems, and your proposed solutions, based on the results you achieved in your past experience. As earnings levels go up in the hierarchy, generalities go down in the interview.

Can you recognize a "courtesy" interview? It usually comes about when one of your key contacts sets it up. The interviewer may politely, even energetically go through the interview, knowing full well he has nothing for you. But, he agrees to talk to you because you both have the mutual acquaintance who arranged the get-together. These interviews, unproductive on the surface, can have value for you. If there is no opening now, perhaps there will be in the unexpected future. Is there any other kind of opportunity you can learn about? Finally, you can ask the interviewer for leads he may know about in other organizations.

When a job offer does arrive, don't jump too fast. Learn all there is to know before you leap. Because if you say "yes" to the wrong employer, you will just have to do the search all over again soon. Find out why the job is open. Did the former incumbent get fired or promoted or what? Why did this happen? Does it pose any problems for you? How about the individuals already in the organization who might have gotten the job in place of you? Can you talk with your predecessor and your new subordinates? Will you be given adequate staff to get the job done?

POSITION CHANGE CONSIDERATIONS: WORK FACTORS

Importance	General Factor	Current Job Rating	Prospective Job Rating
1	Job Interest	_____	_____
1	Importance of Work to the Organization	_____	_____
1	Caliber of Superior	_____	_____
1	Caliber of Co-workers	_____	_____
1	Earnings	_____	_____
1	Relative Position in the Organization	_____	_____
1	Personal Security	_____	_____
1	Relationship to Ownership	_____	_____
1	Workload	_____	_____
1	Pressure—Worry	_____	_____
1	Freedom in Handling Job	_____	_____
2	General Atmosphere	_____	_____
2	Fringe Benefits	_____	_____
2	Travel Required	_____	_____
2	Working Hours—Days	_____	_____
2	Overtime Required	_____	_____
3	Personal Freedom During Working Hours	_____	_____
3	Time for Personal Affairs	_____	_____
3	Personal Office/Work Area	_____	_____
3	Outside Activities	_____	_____
3	Commuting Travel Required	_____	_____

section 12

handling your interviews effectively

Purpose of the Interview

An interview is the formal name for an exchange of information and impressions. It is simply an opportunity for *both* you and the potential employer to begin to get acquainted. It is a mutual checkup on each other, to see if you and position match.

An employer has two basic aims; to get the right person for the job, and to get a person who can contribute something to the organization's goals. So, an interview is not a casual conversation; it is a serious matter. It can be friendly, very cordial . . . but still it's serious.

For any applicant, there are two cardinal rules. Be prepared and be yourself. Your success in a job search may well be determined by how you handle yourself in an interview. Keep in mind that you really have two possibilities of a job from any interview. First, your qualifications may fit you for the position open. Second, an interviewer might try to find a spot for you somewhere, because of your abilities or special talents.

All Kinds of Interviewers

Your interviewer, who may be in Personnel, or who may turn out to be your new boss, can be excellent, well trained, a professional, badly trained, opinionated or a rank amateur. He may be too busy to talk enough to you, or have a lot of extra time for chit-chat. But whatever he is . . . there he is. It's up to you to be alert and handle yourself accordingly. And while reference in this Section is to "He," your interviewer or new boss may very well be "She."

What the Employer Looks For

An employer tries to determine if YOU are the best person with the right qualifications and the finest potential to fill the job. He is evaluating you, so send out the right signals.

He is looking for these things in an employee: (1) a fairly normal human being, mature regardless of age, who is realistic and stable; (2) ability and aptitude; (3) training and experience; (4) willingness to learn and work; (5) congeniality; (6) desire to help create a profit or accomplish the goals.

Special qualities an employer seeks for a Management or Supervisory person will include: (1) previous successful supervision; (2) broad understanding of management; (3) leadership; (4) potential for promotion in management; (6) a career minded person.

What You Can Look For

Foremost, be alert to the opportunity of getting hired. Watch how an interview goes, and sense the interviewer's receptivity.

Learn what you can about the company or organization as the interviewer tries to *sell* you on the idea of employment there. Does it do something worthwhile in your eyes? How big is it, or how big is the division or section you will be in? Does the size suit you? Is it financially sound?

In a business situation, is the company progressive, merely going along on a plateau, or is it going down? Where is the whole industry headed?

Learn all you can about your specific position. Will you like this work? Is there enough challenge for you . . . or maybe too much? Will you learn something valuable? Will this position lead to something bigger?

As a general practice, don't worry about the benefits and working conditions on the first interview. Let this information come out when you've had an offer. No interviewer looks favorably on an applicant who devotes his early questions to: "What can the employer do for me?"

The overall question to be settled in your mind is this: "Is most everything right about the organization, and will I fit in, and will I enjoy what the position offers?"

Prepare Yourself for the Interview

Know yourself! Be thoroughly acquainted with your complete work and educational history, and particularly with what you've said in your resume. It's good to carry a couple of resumes along, in case your interviewer calls for one.

Practicing for an interview isn't a bad idea. Set up a practice session at home before you go on an interview. It can help to have several actual interviews, even on jobs you don't want or know you can't get, just for the practice.

It is very helpful to know enough about the organization interviewing you so that you can discuss the matters at hand with a background knowledge. For example, you need to know items like these: correct name and address; general field or industry; products or services; kinds of clients or customers; distribution methods; sales or activity volume; number of employees.

Types of Interviews/Interview Divisions

All interviews are not of the same kind. Just so you'll know, here are some of the various ones: Screening (preliminary or first); In-depth (first or second); Patterned or structured; Psychological; Multiple (several interviewers); Group (numerous applicants at once); Social; Telephone; Stress.

An interview can often be divided into four areas. Usually, the first half belongs to the interviewer. He sets the tone of the interview. Your job is to offer the information requested. Be concise. Be responsive but not a compulsive talker. The second half offers you the opportunity to supply additional relevant material to convince the interviewer.

Part one is the introduction, a time to get acquainted and put both parties at ease. Next is the questioning by the interviewer, so he can make an evaluation. He wants to learn what you can do for the organization. Listen for clues as to his problems. Keep your replies positive and brief at this point. Not "yes" or "no" but simple. Don't digress. The third part is where you begin to sell yourself. Explain how you could help solve his problems. Show why you like this kind of work. Show your interest in the job. Part four is the closing. Ask for the job, if you want it. Let the interviewer bring up the subject of salary. If he doesn't, you might say: "Could we discuss the salary for this position?" If no final decision is indicated by the interviewer, or if he will be seeing other people, find out the exact day and time you can call him. Ask when you would start, if hired.

When Is the Interview Over?

The interviewer decides when it's over. Watch him for signs. His voice or choice of words may indicate the approaching end of the interview. He may look at his watch once or twice. If he rises from his chair, it's a sure sign. He might put away his glasses. He may stop taking notes. For your part, don't stretch out the interview. Don't keep on talking. However, don't let any loose ends hang. Find out who will call whom, and when. Then thank the interviewer and leave promptly.

Suggestions on How to Conduct Yourself

It is important to act natural and just be yourself. Since first impressions often carry a lot of weight, consciously or otherwise, watch your appearance and posture. A first impression won't get you the job, but may lose it for you. Your clothes should be suitable for the position you hope to get, and on the conservative side. Good grooming is a must.

For an interview, don't arrive too early but definitely not late. Be a smiling person, but don't try and relate too much, especially with the receptionist or the interviewer's secretary. Jokes are out of order. Be patient . . . don't fidget or be irritated.

Your attitude can mean a lot. Be pleasant, normal, easy to talk to . . . no role-playing, just be yourself. It pays to present yourself as confident and successful.

Show an interest in the interviewer and what he is saying. In speaking about past employers, say only good things.

A word about smoking. The best advice is *don't*. Keep your voice modulated but be quietly enthusiastic. Try to sell yourself without being the least bit pushy. Listen most of the time. Be serious, but adjust to the tone of the interview, and to the atmosphere set by the interviewer.

What are your two key tasks? First, to sell yourself; second, to get the job if you want it. Say that you can handle the job, but don't say you can handle it easily. Always tell the truth. Don't interrupt the interviewer. If you don't know the answer to a question, say so. Don't bluff. Don't discuss your personal, domestic, or financial problems unless you are specifically asked about them.

Success depends a lot on how you conduct yourself during an interview. Are you a poised person? Can you relate to an interviewer in what he would consider a normal manner? It's a combination of what you do, how you act, how you appear, how you talk, and what your education/training/experience have been.

The interviewer will let you talk over half the time. He listens. He wants to find what happened to you in your education or experience so far; more importantly, why it happened. He tries to learn whether you really want to succeed, or merely want to avoid failure.

Things the Interviewer May Ask or Discuss

Work Experience:

1. Duties and responsibilities of present and previous positions.
2. Work demands in terms of precision, accuracy, quantity, reaction to emergencies, dealing with other people, creativity, closeness of supervision.
3. Jobs and work demands liked and disliked.
4. Reasons for changing jobs—continuity of employment—reasons for gaps in employment.
5. Evaluation of past employees, supervisor, management, and organization.
6. Reasons for choosing occupation—type of work preferred in terms of duties, responsibilities, salary, work demands.

Educational Training:

1. Schools attended, subjects taken, grades, degrees (dates) and honors obtained.
2. Extracurricular activities (extent and nature)—summer and part-time employment.
3. Reasons for choice of school and subjects, and activities.

Other Activities:

1. Hobbies and avocational activities—reasons for choices and amount of time spent on them.
2. Participation in social, youth, community, fraternal, and other nonwork groups—extent of participation and reasons for choice—leadership positions held.
3. Extent and nature of reading and studying on subjects not connected with present work.
4. Military record—extent of service, assignments, rank—reaction to military service.

Health:

1. Extent of sick leave—reasons.
2. Need for medical and surgical care at present and in the past.
3. Health of family.

After the Interview

After your interview is completed, it might be very wise to write a note to your interviewer. Not many people do this, so it really can be an effective tool. Your interviewer will be appreciative. Make it a short, sincere note of appreciation and mail it that evening or the next day. Reaffirm your interest in the position and express an interest in meeting with the interviewer again.

Make each interview worthwhile, from a learning standpoint. Ask yourself questions like these: "How did the interview go?"; "What good points did I make?"; "Was I poised and confident?"; "Did I miss any good opportunities?"; "Did I forget to ask about some key factors in the job?"; "Did I talk enough? Too much?"; "Did I do the unforgiveable—interrupt the interviewer?"; "Was I tense?"; "Was I too aggressive—or not aggressive enough?"; "How can I improve my next interview?".

Application Blanks Need Careful Attention

At levels below management or executive status, the completed application form is often what an employer sees before he sees you. Fill it out so that your record, experience and educational training are presented in better form than many applicants think necessary. An employer makes judgements about you from the application. Is it complete? Can he read it easily? Any gaps in your work history? Did you follow exactly the instructions on the form?

How can anyone fill in an application form in twenty minutes? Not hard at all, and without pressure. Simply be fully prepared for it. Have all the facts about your personal data, educational background, work history and references written in a notebook, or added to a copy of your resume. Carry it with you at all times. Make the data complete; names, street addresses, cities, states, zip codes, telephone numbers and dates. Not only about you but about prior employers, schools, colleges, references. Remember your Social Security number and military data. Your record of past salaries or wages should be accurate for amounts and dates.

Suppose that you've had what appears to be a promising interview, and your resume was well received. Then the interviewer may ask you to fill out the application blank "just for the record". He's casual about it. But you shouldn't be. Fill it out with extreme care. Double check it against your resume. Do it promptly. Complete all the blank spaces and do not write "see my resume".

Sometimes an application blank may be longer than usual, and will allow three to twenty lines for you to make some general statements about yourself, your goals and expectations. There might be questions such as: "What are your short-term and long-term goals?"; "Why do you want to work for us?". You need to prepare for such application form requirements in advance. Answer in positive but conservative terms. Talk about contributions which give you job satisfaction, about your expected growth and development, about the reputation of the organization. Don't try to fool an interviewer. Don't talk about money and security.

section 13

how to get that first job

Individuals sometimes get a first "permanent" job immediately after high school graduation. But you can get a first job two years later, after finishing a business or vocational school or junior college. Your search for your first full time, permanent job might begin after college graduation or completion of military service. Or, if you've gone on to advanced degrees, it might be many years after high school. In every case, a first job is a challenge . . . not only to get it, but to get the right job for you.

Start with an Inventory

How can you go about this search? Just begin with you; what do you have to offer? What strong points and assets, what weaknesses? Start by preparing a two column personal inventory. List your strong points, then your negatives.

Make a complete record of your summer, part-time and temporary work experiences and show the functions you handled or position titles you had. Now review your school transcripts and record your principal courses. Add your outside interests, your community services, your leadership activities and military experience. Finally, bring all these together into two concisely worded lists; a plus list and a minus (or absence) list. Ponder these lists because you now know what you have to sell. A potential employer will be doing the very same thing mentally when he interviews you. If you have trouble being fair and objective in making these lists, have someone who knows you well lend a hand. Don't let ego or false modesty spoil the effort.

What Do You Really Want to Do?

Do you want to sell, to record, to calculate, to make, to serve, to persuade or what? Do you want to manage or lead or supervise . . . or are you happier without these responsibilities? You should set a goal, define your objective. Or, perhaps two or three objectives, in order of importance to you. You'll get valuable experience in trying to pin yourself down to answering these questions. What do I want to do? What can I do best to make a contribution?

How's the Market Today?

Now that you know what you have to offer, and what you'd like to do, let's assume you have prepared a good resume accordingly. The next big question is: who will need me?

This is a marketing problem. So make your own personal marketing plan. Are you entering business, a profession, social service or government? The marketing elements are much the same. Techniques and avenues of approach will differ.

If you have the courage, time and finances to go after what YOU want, congratulations! You can thus avoid settling for any job, rather than for "the" job. What is "the" job? It could be the one where you have a contribution to make, where you'll find happiness and satisfaction in using your talents. And, where going to work in the morning is anticipated, not dreaded.

Will You Have Competition for the Job?

You most certainly will have competition. Be prepared for it. But if you have a good resume, good educational and/or military training, a willingness to give 110% and you can wrap up all this in good interviews, you won't have to worry so much about competition.

The key word here is "interviews." You need as many as you can get. With each succeeding one, you should become better at handling yourself. The interview is where you get hired . . . or passed over.

Preparing for the Interview

Since the interview is two-sided, it makes good sense to be well prepared accordingly. Not only for the answers you will want to give to the interviewer's questions, but for the questions you will want to ask. The interviewer's job is to find out about you; your motivations, talents, attitude and ability to fit in and carry a share of the load. Your job is to find out what the position is all about . . . whether it fills your needs for job satisfaction and earnings . . . what the organization offers in future growth potential for you.

So once more, it's time to do your homework in advance. Learn all you can about the employer's products or goals, budgets or sales volume and financial strength before the interview. Any experienced interviewer will have his own set of all-purpose questions. You need your set, too.

Here are three questions you'll be likely to be asked, whether you're an MBA, Ph.D or recent high school graduate . . . so have solid, sensible answers ready:

1. What do you want to do?
2. Why do you want to work for us?
3. Tell me about yourself!

Accepting a Job Offer

Do you accept the first offer? What if it's the only one? How do I decide what to do? How best to handle my acceptance? How long will they wait for my answer? How about the money? All good questions...all need answers. All the guidelines known can't really give you specific answers to these basic questions, because each is personal to you. Each can be answered only if the circumstances surrounding each offer is known.

You simply have to think about all the factors involved with each job offer, write down the reasons for and against, and then decide. But first, ask yourself:

1. Do you and the job match, as you start your career?
2. Will you be proud of the organization?
3. Do you feel that you can get along with and work with your new boss and the other employees?
4. Based on the economic climate of the country and of this organization will the job be reasonably secure?
5. How many solid offers do you have?
6. How badly do you need a job?
7. Is the salary reasonable and fair?

Once you've decided and accepted, stay with your decision and give the new job your best.

section 14

guidelines for current college graduates

If you are a rapidly maturing young person about to graduate from college, you have a remarkably unique opportunity to get a job you want in your field of interest. Make the most of it because circumstances in your life will probably never be exactly the way they are for you today.

As A Person: Your Assets

Have you ever spent several hours listing and objectively considering what you are, what you desire and all you have to offer? Possibly a pleasant surprise awaits you. Consider your personal characteristics, your educational training, whatever work history you have, your extra-curricular activities at school and in your community. Most important, study your personal traits and how they may affect your choice of jobs as well as your ability to succeed in a particular job.

A good way to begin and maintain your personal inventory of assets is to set up a notebook, or a series of file folders, with headings to include personal data, job and career objectives, education, special training, military, work experience, references, hobbies, volunteer activities, awards, professional organizations. A complete inventory of YOU will: (1) bring out factors leading to a job or career objective decision; (2) provide data for a good resume; (3) give you the facts for filling out application forms; (4) prepare you for interview questions; (5) be the start of a continuing record of your assets throughout your working career.

Objective/Planning/Marketing

Career planning and job objective determination need careful thought, and usually good guidance. This subject cannot be considered in full in this GUIDE. However, a brief mention of salient points is in order. To be successful in a career, one important factor is the ability to do the kind of work required in that occupation. Second is the personal drive and enthusiasm on that job, to do it well on a week in—week out basis, and thus implement that basic ability into productive results.

Whether you call it a job search, whether it is organized or not, the long-term goal of your efforts is the right job for you as a person. The short term goal, however, is interviews. Your likelihood of interviews, in addition to those on campus, is in direct proportion to your setting up a marketing plan, and using that plan persistently and effectively. Read Section XI of this GUIDE, and adjust your marketing plan to those avenues open to current graduates. The earlier you make a plan, the better. Waiting until your last semester may be usual, but not nearly as good as doing it sooner. Why wait? Last semester demands on your time and energies are heavy. Besides, you get the jump on your competition.

Your marketing plan includes a comprehensive list of possible employers, consideration of the effective ways to reach the market, your resume, action oriented cover letters, and a follow-up system that works. Plus all the help you can get from individuals who can aid you. Plus, a knowledge of how to fill out application forms and most vital of all, how to handle yourself in interviews. The interview is where it happens —you boost your chances of getting the right job, or you fail. You can fail not because you can't do the work, but because you did not sell yourself to the interviewer. A word about record keeping. Set up a folder for each job contact. Keep copies of your letters, and their letters. List all dates of interviews and phone calls. Build up your collection of data about the organization.

In your overall marketing plan, you will want to include the many organizations who do not recruit on campus; they far exceed in number of those who do. Any one employer, even a giant corporation, must limit recruiting efforts to just a few sources. So set up your market targets to meet your needs, whether they recruit on campus or not. Remember, thousands of small and medium size employers do not have a campus recruiting program.

Looking Over Prospective Employers

Your first job after college graduation may be step one in a career, whether you have planned that lifetime work in advance, or it develops as you continue and progress. So, look over potential employers with care. Learn all you can about each one. Your selection of one can affect your entire working life. If you choose correctly, happiness and job satisfaction can be yours. Your choice should not be bad simply because you did not check it out. Furthermore, getting together this data about an employer could easily be a big plus in the interview. First, the interviewer expects you to know about his organization. If you don't, your lack of interest or initiative is a negative. Second, what you learn in advance saves just that much time in the interview. You've only got 20 to 30 minutes, so make them produce for you.

Here are some things to check on and consider:

1. The organization: Does it do something worthwhile in your eyes? Will you be proud to work here? Does it have a good and deserved reputation? Financially sound? Going up or down? Where is the industry or the field going?

2. Location: Do I want to work in this geographical location? Where are the other plants or offices or regional headquarters? How does my family react to this (or another) area?

3. Size: What actually is the size of the unit I am considering? Do I want a large or a small organization, company or agency? Is the total size too big, so I may get lost? Or do I want size, for growth potential?

4. Age: Has it been established for years? Long enough? Too long?

5. Services/Products/Goals: Do I really know what this employer does? What other divisions or branches do? Does it do these things well?

6. Organization structure: What are my promotional steps? Will the job I am considering be dead-end? Will I have exposure where it counts? How fast do their employees move up?

Preparing for an Interview

The interview has as its purpose the exchange of information and impressions, so that you and the employer can reach a decision whether or not to proceed with the employment process. It is a mutual checkup to see if you and the position match. How important is it to be ready and prepared for the interview? Just this: the hiring decision is made either during an interview, or some time thereafter, based to great extent on what you said and how you acted. So be ready!

Consider these two goals for yourself in the interview: (1) sell yourself; (2) get the job. And, in that order. The employer's goals include: (1) get the right person for the job; (2) get a person who can (and will) contribute to the organization's goals. Remember the two cardinal rules for successful interviewing: (1) be prepared; (2) be yourself. Being prepared involves both knowing all about yourself, based on your personal inventory of assets and knowing all you can about the organization, as outlined above. Few interviews are successful where the graduate doesn't know what he wants.

Knowing the usual interview routine will help you to prepare. For specifics, see Section XII on "Types of Interviews/Interview Divisions". Any interviewer may change the pattern or the pace; every interviewer has certain personal methods or variations. Here are three simple but important practices for you to follow: (1) know the exact place and time of the interview and carry a written notation of this with you; (2) know the full name of the organization and its address; (3) know your interviewer's full name, and how to correctly pronounce it.

The Campus Interview

Here is where you must make that good first impression, where you must handle yourself well. A good first impression may not get you the job, but a bad impression could destroy you right there. How you act and dress can be about as important as what you tell the interviewer. Here are specific recommendations on handling yourself in an interview: dress in good taste, on the conservative side; be clean and well groomed; arrive 10 minutes early but never late; greet the interviewer by name; follow his lead or cues; in shaking hands, use a firm grip; show an interest in the interviewer; be responsive to questions; sit up straight; always tell the truth; don't lean on or touch anything on the desk or table; don't smoke; don't put the interviewer on the spot; don't interrupt the interviewer; do not bluff; be prepared for the interviewer's probable questions; have your own questions thought out.

What can you look for? Keep uppermost in mind one thing—the opportunity to get hired. Look for the ways to answer the interviewer's two basic questions: (1) what you can offer the organization; (2) why you are interested. Be alert to what an interviewer tells you about his organization, so you can make a judgement. Do not expect to get hired during a campus interview. The interviewer is screening you to determine if there should be a home base interview. Look for signs to see if you can determine how the interview is going.

The employer also looks, and looks hard. The interviewer must try, even in this screening process, to determine if you are the best person with the right qualifications and the finest potential to fill the job. He is evaluating all the time. In summation, he looks for a fairly normal human being, preferably with a sound background, a maturity regardless of age, a realistic person with a desirable attitude. He looks for aptitude and ability and a willingness to learn and work. He wants a congenial person who will fit into his particular organization.

An interviewer looks for general traits (some of which he cannot judge accurately) such as poise and sense of well being, communications skills, ability to relate well with others, confidence, drive, leadership potential and responsibility acceptance. He may use a rating form with many more traits.

During an interview, on campus or later, be ready for some seemingly unusual questions. You'll do better if you are prepared to give honest, constructive answers to questions such as: "why do you want this job?"; "what do you expect to contribute to our goals?"; "what do you have to offer us?" Some questions can't be answered simply. For some, there are no right answers, so you should anticipate some like these:

"Tell me about yourself". Answer: decide in advance how you will reply. You might smile and just ask in what areas the interviewer would be most interested. Or, begin with an aspect of your objective you enjoy most. Be brief. Wait for the interviewer to pursue that topic or the next one.

"What can I do for you?" Answer: perhaps say: "I'll appreciate all the help you can give me. I want this job. How shall we start to talk about it?"

"What do you expect to be doing five years from now?" Answer: "If I'm hired and the opportunities are as good as I believe them to be, I'll be right here in this organization. But I will expect to be doing more responsible work, with much greater earnings."

Your answers to these questions give the interviewer the opportunity to judge how well you handle unusual situations, how you've planned for the interview, whether you show any drive to progress, whether you get upset easily. He may not pay attention to what specifics you come up with. He is interested in how you field the questions. Remember two basic thoughts in the interviewer's mind: what can you offer to our organization? Do you really want to work for us, and why?

Summing up the matter of what the interviewer looks for in a student applicant, it goes like this: (1) get all the facts possible in this 20 to 30 minute span, to decide whether or not a second company interview is worthwhile; (2) get an overall picture of you as a person as well as a potential employee; (3) see if you know what you want to do, why, and if you have the initiative and determination to probably be successful; (4) get a good handle on your academic achievements in college, and see if they are relevant to your apparent interests or abilities; (5) try and match you, your education and your interests with the work the organization has to offer.

The matter of salary is often not easy to discuss in a short interview. Do you really know at this point what is fair for you, and what you would accept? Many factors enter into your decision. Is this one job your first choice? What if you can't get as much as you want, but the interest and challenge would be great? Look at it from the employer's point of view. How can your value be judged in a preliminary interview? How do you compare to other graduates, from your own school and other schools? How badly does the job need filling? Also, for many entry level/training positions, the employer has an established range (or maximum) which he must adhere to.

Possibly you will be asked how much salary you expect. If you can politely do so, it may be best to pass this question right back to the interviewer. You can normally expect him to press you further. If you have to state something in dollar figures, use a reasonable range and not a flat amount. One reply to the salary question might be that you feel that you expect the going rate. For your part, you will do your very best. Endeavor to sell yourself to the interviewer before the money question arises. If the interviewer wants you, he will make his best offer.

The interview may be terminated, due to time limitations, before either you or the interviewer is finished. Follow his lead. Watch for the signs. Don't keep on talking. If you are interested, say so firmly but briefly. Thank the recruiter for his time and effort, sincerely. Be confident as you leave, even if you did not think that the interview went well. Do not be disappointed or discouraged if no offer of a job or of a certain salary is made. Job offers are not usually forthcoming until further interviews take place.

How should you follow up the interview? First, by learning exactly who is going to make the next contact, as you leave the interview. Then, follow the agreement or instructions exactly. In lieu of a specific time pattern, write the interviewer after one week. Another thank you is in order, and an expression of your continued interest.

One more thought on campus interviews: they are granted and arranged for rather automatically, and cannot be used as the one and only method of getting a job. A campus recruiter who talks to ten students doesn't have ten job openings. It follows that you should not be discouraged by a number of turndowns. Everybody has them!

The Company Visit

In a business situation, for the successful applicant the campus interview is followed by an invitation for one or more visits to a firm's home office, branch or divisional office, or plant. You will usually receive a letter, specifying a certain date, or possibly asking you to choose from among several suggested dates. If you do have a sincere interest in the prospect of working here, accept by phone or letter. You will not necessarily be talking again with the campus recruiter, but with other individuals. Several officials may spend time with you, and evaluate you as a person, how you handle yourself, and your potential in their eyes. They will be looking to see how you fit in with present employees.

The company will either make arrangements for hotel/motel accommodations or suggest where you should do so. You will likely be expected to make your own travel plans and secure tickets. You will be reimbursed for all your expenses during your travel and your stay. Keep a very careful record and save your receipts. Basic rule is to travel reasonably well, but without excesses. For example, do not buy a first class air fare ticket. Don't be cheap but don't live it up. Above all, be honest on the expense account. The company may well evaluate you on your judgement in handling expenses. You may be reimbursed before you leave, or later by mail. Best to have your own travel fund cash with you for any emergencies. Should you visit two or more companies on the same trip, split the expenses fairly, and explain to each exactly how you did it.

A company visit not only allows them to look you over, but lets you look them over. And that's the way they intend it. You can evaluate the company management, the employees, the geographical area and the job. You should ask questions, get several viewpoints. Find out about promotional possibilities, transfer likelihood, benefits, housing, community resources of interest to you.

How and when does a company make a job offer? Usually by phone or letter, and within a reasonable time after your company visit. In return, they expect you to decide promptly, usually within a week or so. If you need more time, ask them but abide by their answer. If you need their decision on you, because of another job offer, call them and explain the circumstances.

Once you've accepted a job, further interviews with other companies are not in order. When you make a decision, stay with it. Write a note to all other firms, thanking them and telling them that you have accepted a position. Even if you should receive another job offer, turn it down. That is how you expect to be treated by any company making you an offer. An offer made in good faith and accepted in good faith should be considered settled by both parties.

Your Placement Director/Career Counselor

Give your Placement Director a chance to help you, but don't expect anyone else to do your work for you, or take charge of your marketing plan. Do not expect more than your Placement Director can deliver, for many good reasons. The number of students involved, the other demands of Placement and Counseling, the usually limited budget and sometimes the size of the staff may all prevent a Placement Director from making an intensive personal effort on your behalf. Guidance, counseling and assistance are available to some degree at almost every school and college, but getting the job is strictly up to you.

A final recommendation: get to know your Placement Director/Career Counselor early in your college career. You will have more time to consider alternatives and make decisions. Checking out your fields of interest and securing data on individual organizations can be done less hastily. When campus interviewing time arrives, you'll be better prepared.

section 15

overcoming handicaps in your job search

You have a handicap, do you, which could hurt your job search? Well, who doesn't? Of course you may have a certain handicap but so do most people. Sometimes the handicap is apparent, sometimes not. Neither you nor anyone else is going to be fully acceptable to everyone. While you could ignore the problem, you can frequently make an asset of it.

Guidelines for Turning Adversity Into Opportunity

You will need to have an even better resume. You will want to be more persistent in your search. Place more emphasis on what you do best: talent, ability, experience.

Remember: often it is not your handicap that is against you . . . it is your mental attitude about it. So turn around that attitude and convince yourself it can be done, because it really can!

Be objective about yourself. Disregard your race, color, age, experience defects, lack of education, or whatever your so-called handicap may be. You have something to offer, so go after that next job with all the positive attitude you can develop.

The Age Factor

When people normally refer to age as a handicap, they think in terms of over 60 or over 50. Actually, being too young can be called a handicap also. You can very well be a top caliber manager, woman or man, at age 28, which may just mean that you have learned in 3 years what most people experience in 7 years. Some employers may reject you because of immaturity or lack of experience. What they are really saying is: "too young." Your resume can overcome resistance by stressing achievements, current position title and earnings level.

If "youth" is not your problem, and an older age seems to be, then recognize the fact that finding a job is going to be hard work. It may take more drive, more time, more patience, and more effort than usual. But also recognize that it can be done . . . it is being done every day by thousands of job seekers.

Why should a potential employer view an older person as a poor candidate for a position? He might feel that your experience is too great for his job; he may believe you to be too expensive or set in your ways; he may wonder why it is you are looking for a new job or re-entering the market. He is probably wrong much of the time, but you need to show him how you are the exception. Sell yourself to him by emphasizing experience and mature judgement.

In an interview, just don't dwell on your age. An interviewer quickly detects it if you are overly concerned with it. About your specific age, say as little as possible. Touch on it quickly if asked, then go immediately to some positive aspect of your abilities or experience. Better to refrain from making a speech about age discrimination. Your purposes in the interview are to sell yourself and get the job, not establish your private feelings about moral and legal questions. Be confident about what maturity has given you.

You may have advantages over youth. Use them in a discussion, but never argue about them. You usually can point to a greater understanding of other human beings; greater or broader experience, either in supervision or working with others; more experience in making correct judgements or decisions. One caution: avoid overly long discussions of a point, even though you have had much experience. If an interviewer wants to know more details, he'll ask.

Experience, Employment History and Present Status

What if you haven't any experience at all, or only summer and part-time jobs? Then you will want to stress the plus factors you possess...your educational training, military experience if relevant, your strong desire, your willingness to work hard.

You can have a lot of experience...years of it, and discover that it's too narrow, too general, or perhaps you gained it all with one or two companies in a single kind of work. What's needed here is a careful analysis of exactly what you know and do well, and restate it. Be honest, as always, but look at yourself to see what can be stressed toward a new situation. Convey the feeling of how this lengthy experience can solve problems and get the job done for a new organization.

Looking back over your career, does it appear that you've had too many jobs? Have potential employers said as much to you? Here is where a functional or analytical type of resume may serve better than a chronological presentation. Yet, having had many jobs can be an asset. They have given you a broader exposure to different kinds of situations, different industries or fields, and probably many more people to deal with.

What if you are unemployed or soon will be? On the plus side, you do have the necessary days and hours to work on your job search full time. What's needed here is strong determination and a willingness to work very hard on the search. Waste no time getting started, once you've decided on what kind of a job you want. Explore all the avenues open to you. Another plus may be your immediate availability. The new organization doesn't have to wait 3 or 4 weeks before you start.

Education: Too Little or Too Much

Education is a bit like experience, in that you can have not enough, or with a fine educational background, too little in a particular field. This problem is quite common, so don't worry about it. You can't change it overnight, so see how what you do have can become helpful in your current search. As a forward step, one that makes you more employable, you can enroll toward a new degree, or take the necessary courses, in Evening Divisions or Adult Continuing Education programs.

Some employers demand a degree, or an advanced degree. If you don't have equivalent experience, you are up against a real road block. However, make an effort to get interviews anyway. It is possible you can sell yourself, and many people have. Often, a smaller size organization will be more flexible.

Sex, Race, National Origin, Physical Condition

Yes, some people will discriminate against you for these factors...or for dozens of other personal prejudices. We are all prejudice-laden. It is an established fact, however, that these biases are disappearing; not only because of the laws now on the books, but down deep in the hearts of people. When we begin to know other people, lose our fear of a different colored skin, and understand somewhat another person's culture, our prejudice becomes less important to us.

Best advice seems to be to proceed with your job search in a normal way, and assume that a potential employer will indeed consider you for what you have to offer. Do not be defensive. You'll probably have to work harder, if any of these factors prove to be actual handicaps in your own case.

If you have a physical handicap, and it's minor, don't mention it on your resume. Do include it in any application blank, however, if called for. What is necessary to do is to present yourself to a potential employer on the strength of what you can do well, what you can contribute to the organization. If your physical needs demand certain working conditions, you'll have to cover this in your interview. Employers are not happy with surprises your first day on the job.

You have no doubt accepted your particular physical handicap as a fact of life. An employer will, too, and will count on you as a productive employee, just as he does anyone else on the staff.

Good first impressions are always important, in any interview, for any job seeker. If you have (or feel that you have) a handicap, then a favorable first impression is vital. Come across as a personable individual. If you do it right, and sell yourself first, potential or actual handicaps tend to disappear in the mind of the interviewer.

Termination Problems and Recommendations

Many "sudden terminations" aren't really that sudden, and probably should have been foreseen. Be alert to any handwriting on the wall. Small at first, it often has a cumulative effect, and the handwriting gets plainer and plainer. Sometimes everybody can read it except the potential victim. He either buries his head, or insists that it can't happen to him. But it can, and does. In the end, the ax falls.

If you even suspect that your job loss is imminent, or even possible, begin your job search at once. Otherwise, when termination day arrives, your problem is bigger than it has to be. Two common effects of a termination are panic, and doing everything wrong in the job search. Being objective about your own job security, and watching for the signs help you avoid these disasters.

But fear of job loss, well founded or only a false rumor, is very unsettling. It's a soul searing, enervating, crippling state of mind. So do not try to just live with it. Decide whether to confront your boss and try and get the facts, or decide to begin your search immediately. Either way, you'll be healthier and happier. Talk to your superior. If you are not going to get fired, you may get solid assurances. If the matter is being weighed by your management, your boss may still give you assurance; in this case, you decide whether to fight for your job, or make immediate plans yourself. Read between the lines. Sometimes your boss will level with you privately, but often he simply can't afford to do it.

For a number of reasons, it is usually easier to get a job when you have one than when you don't. Psychologically, you are better able to search while you have your normal confidence in yourself and your ego hasn't been shattered. Likewise, employers seem to want to interview employed people. Executives often have a particularly bad time, because they are wholly unaccustomed to being out of work. A majority of people do suffer some degree of shock at either the prospects of termination or the firing itself. There are, however, a number of things you can do, which alleviate the shock condition. There are some steps you must take, and some you should not.

Why get too excited? Easier to say than do, but don't panic, don't bore all your friends, family and co-workers with the details. Why spend hours explaining to people that the management or your boss was wrong. Better to regain your composure and then spend the time on planning your search. These panicky, resentment-driven hours do not hurt your employer's peace of mind, but they erode yours. The inside of you just keeps churning and churning. It is not worth it; besides, you will not starve and your world will not end. Don't figure out a neat little plan to get even with your boss. You might want a good reference from him.

What you should do is (1) nothing whatsoever until you've had a day or two, even a week, to recover from the shock; (2) begin to gather the material for a personal inventory of yourself, your abilities, education, experience and achievements to guide you in your search and to form the basis of your resume; (3) do your work in top-notch fashion if you are still on the job. Your boss remembers very clearly what you did and your attitude during these last weeks or days. He especially remembers if your work was poor and your attitude made him look bad. So be positive. You have much to gain.

Now, plan your job search campaign. Produce the best sales tool you can— your resume. Here are some common sense rules to follow:

1. Maintain the best positive attitude about yourself and your job hunting activities.

2. Get started right away...do not mull over it for weeks or take a vacation first.

3. Make your search, if unemployed, a full time job. Apply your best skills, energy, and knowledge to the search, just as you would to a job.

4. Prepare a very broad marketing plan, and make the maximum number of contacts.

5. Rethink your willingness to relocate, even if you would really prefer to remain in your present area.

6. Keep earnings sights high. Don't talk about salary, especially any lower salary, in a first interview.

7. Enlist the support of your family, in the understanding and cooperation needed to bring success.

appendix

REFERENCE BOOKS FOR EMPLOYER LIST PREPARATION

Among the leading reference books available in public libraries are the following:

DUN AND BRADSTREET MILLION DOLLAR DIRECTORY
Published by Dun and Bradstreet, Inc., New York, New York.
31,000 businesses with $1 million or more in net worth.
Company names, individual names and titles
Sections: Companies alphabetically, geographically, and by
   product classifications.

DUN AND BRADSTREET MIDDLE MARKET DIRECTORY
Published by Dun and Bradstreet, Inc., New York, New York.
30,000 businesses with net worth between $500,000 and $1 million.
Company names, individual names and titles
Sections: Companies alphabetically, geographically, and by
   product classifications.

THOMAS REGISTER OF AMERICAN MANUFACTURERS
Published by Thomas Publishing Co., New York, New York.
National list of 75,000 manufacturers; 80,000 product headings;
   home offices, branches, outlets.
Classified by product, by state, by city, by company.

POOR'S REGISTER OF CORPORATIONS, DIRECTORS & EXECUTIVES
Published by Standard and Poor's Corporation, New York, N. Y.
Corporate listings of 34,000 nationally known companies, with titles
of all leading officers and executives, and individual names. Includes
Standard Industrial Classifications numbers.

STATE INDUSTRIAL DIRECTORIES
Published by Manufacturers News, Inc., Chicago, Illinois.
Available for most states, geographical regions and Canada.

STANDARD DIRECTORY OF ADVERTISERS
Published by National Register Publishing Company, Skokie, Illinois.
Company names, individual names and titles, and Advertising
Agencies serving the companies

STANDARD DIRECTORY OF ADVERTISING AGENCIES
Published by National Register Publishing Company, Skokie, Illinois.
Agency names, individual names and titles

POLK'S BANK DIRECTORY
Published by R. L. Polk & Company, Nashville, Tennessee.
Complete listing of banks, by state, size, individual names and titles.

EXECUTIVE SEARCH FIRMS

California

Billington, Fox & Ellis, Inc.
3701 Wilshire Boulevard
Los Angeles, California 90005

Boyden Associates, Inc.
5670 Wilshire Boulevard
Los Angeles, California 90036

William H. Clark Associates, Inc.
555 South Flower Street
Los Angeles, California 90071

Heidrick & Struggles, Inc.
Union Bank Square
445 South Figueroa Streets
Los Angeles, California 90071

Boyden Associates, Inc.
1 Maritime Plaza
Golden Gateway Center
San Francisco, California 94111

Heidrick & Struggles, Inc.
600 Montgomery Street
San Francisco, California 94111

Ward Howell Associates, Inc.
Three Embarcadero Center
San Francisco, California 94111

Georgia

Billington, Fox & Ellis, Inc.
250 Piedmont Avenue, N.E.
Atlanta, Georgia 30308

Boyden Associates, Inc.
Lennox Towers
3390 Peachtree Road, N.E.
Atlanta, Georgia 30326

Illinois

Billington, Fox & Ellis, Inc.
20 North Wacker Drive
Chicago, Illinois 60606

Boyden Associates, Inc.
10 South Riverside Plaza
Chicago, Illinois 60606

William H. Clark Associates, Inc.
200 East Randolph Drive
Chicago, Illinois 60601

De Voto & Berry Partners, Ltd.
120 South Riverside Plaza
Chicago, Illinois 60606

Eastman & Beaudine, Inc.
111 West Monroe Street
Chicago, Illinois 60603

Heidrick & Struggles, Inc.
125 South Wacker Drive
Chicago, Illinois 60606

Helmich, Miller & Pasek, Inc.
O'Hare Plaza-Suite 635
5725 East River Road
Chicago, Illinois 60631

Hodge, Cronin & Associates, Inc.
9575 W. Higgins Road
Rosemont, Illinois 60018

Edwin C. Johnson & Associates
919 North Michigan Avenue
Chicago, Illinois 60611

James M. Kittleman & Associates,
Inc.
209 South LaSalle Street
Chicago, Illinois 60604

Lamson Griffiths & Parsons
20 North Wacker Drive
Chicago, Illinois 60606

Spencer Stuart Associates,. Inc.
500 North Michigan Avenue
Chicago, Illinois 60611

Spriggs & Company
875 North Michigan Avenue
Chicago, Illinois 60611

Sullivan Associates
20 North Wacker Drive
Chicago, Illinois 60606

Tully & Hobart, Inc.
919 North Michigan Avenue
Chicago, Illinois 60611

Ward Howell Associates, Inc.
875 North Michigan Avenue
Chicago, Illinois 60611

Wytmar & Company, Inc.
10 South Riverside Plaza
Chicago, Illinois 60606

Massachusetts

Thomas A. Buffum Associates
2 Center Plaza
Boston, Massachusetts 02108

Heidrick & Struggles, Inc.
100 Federal Street
Boston, Massachusetts 02110

New York

Antell, Wright & Nagel
230 Park Avenue
New York, New York 10017

Battalia, Lotz and Associates, Inc.
342 Madison Avenue
New York, New York 10017

Billington, Fox & Ellis, Inc.
529 Fifth Avenue
New York, New York 10017

Boyden Associates, Inc.
260 Madison Avenue
New York, New York 10016

William H. Clark Associates, Inc.
330 Madison Avenue
New York, New York 10017

Thorndike Deland Associates
1440 Broadway
New York, New York 10018

Devine, Baldwin & Peters, Inc.
250 Park Avenue
New York, New York 10017

Haskell & Stern Associates, Inc.
230 Park Avenue
New York, New York 10017

Heidrick & Struggles, Inc.
245 Park Avenue
New York, New York 10017

Edward H. Lubin Associates
300 East 54th Street
New York, New York 10022

Joseph L. Rodgers & Company
155 East 38th Street
New York, New York 10016

Spencer Stuart & Associates
437 Madison Avenue
New York, New York 10022

Staub, Warmbold & Associates, Inc.
655 Third Avenue
New York, New York 10017

L. W. Stern Associates, Inc.
95 Madison Avenue, Suite 1408
New York, New York 10016

L. F. Stowell Associates, Inc.
135 East 54th Street
New York, New York 10022

Ward Howell Associates, Inc.
99 Park Avenue
New York, New York 10016

Ohio

Billington, Fox & Ellis, Inc.
1717 East 9th Street
Cleveland, Ohio 44114

Heidrick & Struggles, Inc.
1100 Superior Avenue
Cleveland, Ohio 44114

Pennsylvania

Boyden Associates, Inc.
625 Stanwix Street
Pittsburgh, Pennsylvania 15222

Texas

Billington, Fox & Ellis, Inc.
One Main Place
Dallas, Texas 75250

Boyden Associates, Inc.
2001 Kirby Drive
Houston, Texas 77019

Heidrick & Struggles, Inc.
2650 Pennzoil Place
Houston, Texas 77002

Canada

The Caldwell Partners
50 Prince Arthur Avenue
Toronto, Ontario M5R 1B5

The Caldwell Partners
500 Fourth Avenue, S.W.
Calgary. Alberta T2P 2V6

Currie, Coopers & Lybrand, Ltd.
630 Dorchester Boulevard, West
Montreal, Quebec H3B 1W5

Currie, Coopers & Lybrand, Ltd.
145 King Street West
Toronto, Ontario M5H 1J8

Currie, Coopers & Lybrand, Ltd.
99 Bank Street, Suite 727
Ottawa, Ontario K1P 6B9

Currie, Coopers & Lybrand, Ltd.
1400-639 5th Avenue, S.W.
Calgary, Alberta T2P 0M9

Currie, Coopers & Lybrand, Ltd.
1055 W. Georgia Street Royal
  Center
Vancouver, B.C. V6E 3R2

Currie, Coopers & Lybrand, Ltd.
500 Chancery Hall
Edmonton, Alberta T5J 2C3

Stevenson & Kellogg, Ltd.
2300 Yonge Street
Toronto, Ontario M4P 1G2

Stevenson & Kellogg, Ltd.
1143 Sun Life Building
Montreal, Quebec H3B 2V6

Stevenson & Kellogg, Ltd.
112 West Pender Street
Vancouver, B.C. V6E 2S1

Stevenson & Kellogg, Ltd.
809 Royal Bank Buidling
Winnipeg, Manitoba R3C 0A5

Stevenson & Kellogg, Ltd.
130 Albert Street
Ottawa, Ontario K1P 5G4

Stevenson & Kellogg, Ltd.
760 Elveden House
Calgary, Alberta T2P 0Z3

Woods, Gordon & Co.
253 Royal Trust Tower
Toronto, Ontario M5K 1J7

Woods, Gordon & Co.
160 Elgin Street
Ottawa, Ontario K2P 2CR

Woods, Gordon & Co.
1800 One Lakeview Square
Winnipeg, Manitoba R3C 1K8

Woods, Gordon & Co.
10025 Jasper Avenue
Edmonton, Alberta T5J 1T2

Woods, Gordon & Co.
630 Dorchester Boulevard West
Montreal, Quebec H3B 1T9

Woods, Gordon & Co.
850 Elveden House
Calgary, Alberta T2P 0Z3

Woods, Gordon & Co.
700 West Georgia Street
Vancouver, B.C. V7Y 1C7

MANAGEMENT CONSULTING FIRMS

California

Booz, Allen & Hamilton, Inc.
523 West 6th Street
Los Angeles, California 90014

Booz, Allen & Hamilton, Inc.
555 California Street
San Francisco, California 94104

Cresap, McCormick & Paget, Inc.
650 California Street
San Francisco, California 94108

A. T. Kearney & Company, Inc.
One Wilshire Building
Los Angeles, California 90017

Lester B. Knight & Associates, Inc.
560 Mission Street
San Francisco, California 94105

Georgia

Booz, Allen & Hamilton, Inc.
229 Peachtree St., N.E.
Atlanta, Georgia 30303

Illinois

Gordon H. Anderson & Associates
77 West Washington Street
Chicago, Illinois 60602

Associated Business Consultants
17 East Chestnut Street
Chicago, Illinois 60611

Booz, Allen & Hamilton, Inc.
135 South LaSalle Street
Chicago, Illinois 60603

Case and Company, Inc.
Prudential Plaza
Chicago, Illinois 60601

Cresap, McCormick & Paget, Inc.
30 North LaSalle Street
Chicago, Illinois 60603

Fry Consultants, Inc.
230 North Michigan Avenue
Chicago, Illinois 60601

Robert H. Hayes & Associates, Inc.
20 North Wacker Drive
Chicago, Illinois 60606

A. T. Kearney & Company, Inc.
100 South Wacker Drive
Chicago, Illinois 60606

Lester B. Knight & Associates, Inc.
549 West Randolph Street
Chicago, Illinois 60606

Albert Ramond & Associates, Inc.
435 North Michigan Avenue
Chicago, Illinois 60611

John Paisios & Associates
2222 Kensington Court
Oak Brook, Illinois 60521

Missouri

Lawrence-Leiter & Company
427 West 12th Street
Kansas City, Missouri 64105

New York

Booz, Allen & Hamilton, Inc.
245 Park Avenue
New York, New York 10017

Frank C. Brown & Company, Inc.
342 Madison Avenue
New York, New York 10017

Case and Company, Inc.
30 Rockefeller Plaza
New York, New York 10020

Cresap, McCormick & Paget, Inc.
245 Park Avenue
New York, New York 10017

Drake, Sheahan/Stewart Dougall,
Inc.
330 Madison Avenue
New York, New York 10017

Fairbanks Associates, Inc.
509 Madison Avenue
New York, New York 10022

William E. Hill & Company, Inc.
640 Fifth Avenue
New York, New York 10019

A. T. Kearney & Company, Inc.
437 Madison Avenue
New York, New York 10022

Lester B. Knight & Associates, Inc.
468 Park Avenue, South
New York, New York 10016

Norris & Elliott, Inc.
270 Greenwich Avenue
Greenwich, Connecticut 06830

Albert Ramond & Associates, Inc.
405 Lexington Avenue
New York, New York 10017

Ohio

Booz, Allen & Hamilton, Inc.
1100 Chester Avenue
Cleveland, Ohio 44115

A. T. Kearney & Company, Inc.
1801 East 9th Street
Cleveland, Ohio 44114

Trundle Consultants
5501 South Marginal Road
Cleveland, Ohio 44103

Norris & Elliott, Inc.
85 E. Gay Street
Columbus, Ohio 43215

Pennsylvania

Booz, Allen & Hamilton, Inc.
400 Market Street
Philadelphia, Pennsylvania 19106

Maynard Research Council, Inc.
300 Alpha Drive
Pittsburgh, Pennsylvania 19238

Texas

Booz, Allen & Hamilton, Inc.
325 North St. Paul
Dallas, Texas 75201

Washington, D.C.

Booz, Allen & Hamilton, Inc.
1025 Connecticut Avenue, N.W.
Washington, D.C. 20036

CPA CONSULTING FIRMS

California

Arthur Andersen & Company
1320 West 3rd Street
Los Angeles, California 90017

Coopers & Lybrand
1000 West 6th Street
Los Angeles, California 90017

Ernst & Whinney
515 South Flower Street
Los Angeles, California 90005

Alexander Grant & Company
611 West 6th Street
Los Angeles, California 90005

DeLoitte Haskins & Sells
One Wilshire Building
P.O. Box 60250
Los Angeles, California 90060

Peat Warwick Mitchell & Company
555 South Flower Street
Los Angeles, California 90071

Price Waterhouse & Company
606 South Olive Street
Los Angeles, California 90014

Arthur Young & Company
615 South Flower Street
Los Angeles, California 90071

Arthur Andersen & Company
1 Market Plaza
San Francisco, California 94108

Coopers & Lybrand
One Bush Street
San Francisco, California 94104

Touche Ross & Company
Alcoa Building—One Maritime
    Plaza
San Francisco, California 94411

Georgia

Ernst & Whinney
3600 First National Bank Tower
2 Peachtree Street, N.W.
Atlanta, Georgia 30303

Touche Ross & Company
225 Peachtree Street, N.E.
Atlanta, Georgia 30303

Illinois

Arthur Andersen & Company
69 West Washington
Chicago, Illinois 60602

Coopers & Lybrand
222 S. Riverside Plaza
Chicago, Illinois 60606

Ernst & Whinney
150 South Wacker Drive
Chicago, Illinois 60606

Alexander Grant & Company
Prudential Plaza
Chicago, Illinois 60601

DeLoitte Haskins & Sells
200 E. Randolph Drive
Chicago, Illinois 60601

Peat Marwick Mitchell & Company
222 South Riverside Plaza
Chicago, Illinois 60606

Price Waterhouse & Company
200 E. Randolph Drive
Chicago, Illinois 60601

Touche Ross & Company
111 East Wacker Drive
Chicago, Illinois 60601

Arthur Young & Company
One IBM Plaza
Chicago, Illinois 60610

Massachusetts

Peat Marwick Mitchell & Co.
One Boston Place
Boston, Massachusetts 02108

Arthur Young & Company
1 Boston Place
Boston, Massachusetts 02102

Michigan

Arthur Andersen & Company
400 Renaissance Center
Detroit, Michigan 48243

Coopers & Lybrand
211 West Fort
Detroit, Michigan 48075

DeLoitte Haskins & Sells
100 Renaissance Center
Detroit, Michigan 48243

Ernst & Whinney
100 Renaissance Center
Detroit, Michigan 48243

Alexander Grant & Company
City National Bank Building
Detroit, Michigan 48226

Haskins & Sells
1200 Guardian Building
Detroit, Michigan 48226

Peat Marwick Mitchell & Company
200 Renaissance Center
Detroit, Michigan 48243

Price Waterhouse & Company
200 Renaissance Center
Detroit, Michigan 48243

Touche Ross & Company
200 Renaissance Center
Detroit, Michigan 48243

Arthur Young & Company
100 Renaissance Center
Detroit, Michigan 48243

Missouri

Arthur Andersen & Company
911 Main Street
Kansas City, Missouri 64105

DeLoitte Haskins & Sells
2400 Pershing Road
Kansas City, Missouri 64108

Ernst & Whinney
10 Broadway
St. Louis, Missouri 63102

Alexander Grant & Company
1101 Walnut
Kansas City, Missouri 64106

Peat Marwick Mitchell & Company
Commerce Tower
Kansas City, Missouri 64141

Price Waterhouse & Company
Commerce Tower
Kansas City, Missouri 64141

Arthur Young & Company
Ten Main Center
Kansas City, Missouri 64105

New York

Arthur Andersen & Company
1345 Avenue of the Americas
New York, New York 10019

Coopers & Lybrand
1251 Avenue of the Americas
New York, New York 10020

DeLoitte Haskins & Sells
1114 Avenue of the Americas
New York, New York 10036

Ernst & Whinney
153 East 53rd Street
New York, New York 10022

Alexander Grant & Company
605 3rd Avenue
New York, New York 10016

Peat Marwick Mitchell & Company
345 Park Avenue
New York, New York 10022

Price Waterhouse & Company
153 East 53rd Street
New York, New York 10022

Touche Ross & Company
1633 Broadway
New York, New York 10019

Arthur Young & Company
277 Park Avenue
New York, New York 10017

Ohio

Ernst & Whinney
1300 Union Commerce Building
Cleveland, Ohio 44115

Texas

Peat Marwick Mitchell & Company
1500–2001 Bryan Tower
Dallas, Texas 75201

Ernst & Whinney
2700 LTV Tower
1600 Pacific Avenue
Dallas, Texas 75201

Ernst & Whinney
3500 One Shell Plaza
Houston, Texas 77002

Price Waterhouse & Company
1200 Milam Street
Houston, Texas 77002

Touche Ross & Company
1200 Smith Street
Houston, Texas 77002

Canada

Arthur Andersen & Company
800 Dorchester Boulevard, West
Montreal, Quebec H3B 1X9

DeLoitte Haskins & Sells
One Place Villa Marie
Montreal, Quebec H3B 2W3

DeLoitte Haskins & Sells
Box 283, Toronto-Dominion Centre
Toronto, Ontario M5K 1K4

Ernst & Whinney
Commerce Plaza
King Street
Toronto, Ontario M5L 1C6

Peat Marwick Mitchell & Company
Commerce Court West
P.O. Box 31
Toronto, Ontario M5L 1B2

Peat Marwick Mitchell & Company
1155 Dorchester Boulevard, West
Montreal, Quebec H3B 2J9

Price Waterhouse & Company
1200 McGill College
Montreal, Quebec H3B 2G4

Price Waterhouse & Company
Toronto-Dominion Centre
Toronto, Ontario M5K 1G1

Price Waterhouse & Company
255 Albert Street
Ottawa, Ontario K1P 6A9